Italian
SLOW
COOKING

Italian SLOW COOKING

*More than 250 Recipes
for the Electric
Slow Cooker*

Ellen Brown

CIDER MILL
PRESS

BOOK
PUBLISHERS

Kennebunkport, Maine

13-Digit ISBN: 978-1604332643
10-Digit ISBN: 1604332646

This book may be ordered by mail from the publisher. Please include $3.95 for postage and handling.
Please support your local bookseller first!

Books published by Cider Mill Press Book Publishers are available at special discounts for bulk purchases in the United States by corporations, institutions, and other organizations. For more information, please contact the publisher.

Cider Mill Press Book Publishers
"Where good books are ready for press"
12 Port Farm Road
Kennebunkport, Maine 04046

Visit us on the Web!
www.cidermillpress.com

Design by Alicia Freile, Tango Media
Typography: Chaparral Pro, Helvetica Neue and Voluta

Front cover photo courtesy of Getty Images.
Interior images copyright: page 7, Ewa Walicka; page 9, Anthony Shaw Photography; page 13, Robyn Mackenzie; page 14, Pakhnyushcha; page 16, Darren Brode; page 17, svry; page 18, Maja Wasowicz; page 20, svry; page 22, Dzinnik; page 24, svry; page 28, hd connelly; page 30, Iwona Grodzka; page 32, Martin Allinger; page 34, Robin Stewart; page 36, Dusan Zidar; page 38, marco mayer; page 40, Vasil Vasilev; page 44, Elena Elisseeva; page 46, HG Photography; page 50, HLPhoto; page 52, Taratorki; page 56, Ildi Papp; page 58, Ildi Papp; page 60, Martin Turzak; page 62, Luisa Puccini; page 64, Glenn Price; page 66, lsantilli; page 70, PHB.cz (Richard Semik); page 72, photo-oasis; page 74, Viktor1; page 76, Jaimie Duplass; page 78, Bochkarev Photography; page 80, Ragnarock; page 82, Chiyacat; page 84, Anna Hoychuk; page 86, Robyn Mackenzie; page 88, Massimiliano G.; page 92, tommaso lizzul; page 96, CGissemann; page 98, Chiyacat; page 100, Josh Resnick; page 102, Joe Gough; page 104, Paul Binet; page 106, marco mayer; page 108, Francesco83; page 113, Paul Cowan; page 114, across; page 118, Terry Davis; page 120, Olinchuk; page 122, Chris Christou; page 124, Natalia Mylova; page 126, Fedor Kondratenko; page 128, Digivic; page 130, Wiktory; page 134, Magdalena Zurawska; page 135, Cedric Crucke; page 136, Brett Mulcahy; page 138, Shebeko; page 140, HLPhoto; page 142, Robyn Mackenzie; page 144, SCPixBit; page 146, bond girl; page 150, Lorraine Kourafas; page 152, Joe Gough; page 154, Alias Studiot Oy; page 156, marco mayer; page 158, Lorraine Kourafas; page 160, Shebeko; page 164, Rido; page 165, Malgorzata Kistryn; page 166, dovgan; page 168, across; page 172, Robyn Mackenzie; page 174, msheldrake; page 176, Eldred Lim; page 178, msheldrake; page 180, HLPhoto; page 182, Paul Cowan; page 184, Nayashkova Olga; page 186, Brett Mulcahy; page 190, Alias Studiot Oy; page 192, R.Ashrafov; page 194, Oliver Suckling; page 196, marco mayer; page 198, Olga Lyubkina; page 200, Philip Stridh; page 202, stocknadia; page 204, Filipe B. Varela; page 209, Madlen;page 210, Lilyana Vynogradova; page 212, Andi Berger; page 216, Lulu Durand; page 220, Robyn Mackenzie; page 222, Gayvoronskaya_yana; page 224, Lilyana Vynogradova; page 226, Matt Valentine; page 228, Hellen Sergeyeva; page 230, Anna Hoychuk; page 234, studiogi; page 236, PHB.cz (Richard Semik); page 238, sarsmis; page 242, Noam Armonn; page 244, Andrew Horwitz; page 246, Daniel Padavona; page 248, ElenaKor; page 250, David P. Smith; page 252, Olinchuk; page 256, IngridHS; page 258, bonchan; page 260, Teresa Kasprzycka.
All interior images used under license from Shutterstock.com.

Printed in China

1 2 3 4 5 6 7 8 9 0
First Edition

Contents

This book is dedicated to Zahir Dubler Cerami,
the sweetest little guy in the whole world,
and his parents Lisa Cerami and Josh Dubler,
who also bring such joy to my life.

Preface

Food writers are frequently asked "if you had to choose one cuisine, and eat that food only for the rest of your life, what would it be?" And my answer is always Italian. Why? When you're eating Italian food you're not eating one cuisine but many regional cuisines that were very distinct until the late-nineteenth century when the country underwent political unification and modern transportation and communication led to regions learning more about each other—and the foods they ate.

The many regions of Italy are as diverse as the country's geography, from the snow-capped mountains of the Alps in the north to the sandy beaches of the south. Butter is used more in northern regions while olive oil dominates in the south. Bell peppers and onions are used everywhere, but differently. Each region has long-simmered dishes, and those are the ones you'll find in *Italian Slow Cooking*.

Each of these regions has culinary specialties, just as each produces its unique wines. However, the various regional cuisines are united by the use of only the freshest ingredients, as well as handling those ingredients simply and with respect, as they have for generations. While a few restaurants in Italy might be using liquid nitrogen and other tools part and parcel of today's fad of molecular gastronomy, they are the rare exception. Italian food is honest and straightforward.

There's much chatter in the food community today about "slow food," and this all began in Italy in 1986 when Carlo Petrini from Bra, a small town in Piedmont, organized a group to fight McDonald's from opening near the Spanish Steps in Rome. By 1992 offshoots had been planted in other European communities, and the phrase gained universal meaning by the end of the twentieth century to signify the antithesis of "fast food."

This now international movement opposes the standardization of taste and culture. They are against processed foods and believe that "everyone has a fundamental right to the pleasure of good food." By 2004 "slow food" was so well known that Petrini was named one of *Time* magazine's heroes of the year.

There's no better way to enjoy the pleasures of "slow food" than to cook it in a slow cooker. Slow cooking has been around for centuries, even before there were kitchens—or houses for that matter. The first slow cooking was done in pottery, as it is still today. By the fifth century BCE, iron pots holding simmering food were left to cook around the clock in the fire's embers. Cooking slowly has always been part of all regional Italian cuisines.

Although slow cooking was a necessity in the past, today it's a choice. With some advance preparation, busy people like you can enjoy a delicious, homemade meal that cooked without anyone around to watch it.

I'm continually working on ways to make cooking easier and more pleasurable, as well as producing delicious results. You'll find tricks for browning meat under the broiler rather than dirtying a skillet, and how to effortlessly make dishes such as polenta and risotto—at the very heart of Italian cuisine—that require laborious stirring when cooked on the stove instead of in the slow cooker.

If you're new to slow cooker cooking, you're hardly alone, although slow cookers are now found in almost as many kitchens as coffee pots. Back in the early 1970s I received a slow cooker as a wedding present and promptly turned it into a planter because all the recipes written for this appliance, which was relatively new at the time, called for cans of "Cream of Something" soup and other processed foods. I was a "gourmet" cook; not someone who cooked "all-American favorites."

This is the fifth slow cooker cookbook I've written, and I'm adamant that the slow cooker is a best friend for the modern cook who only uses fresh ingredients. After all, that's the way it's done in Italy. And that's what you'll find in *Italian Slow Cooking*.

Buon appetito!

Ellen Brown
Providence, Rhode Island

Chapter 1

Slow Going:

A Guide to Slow Cookers and the Wonders of Slow Cooking

*L*uckily for all of us who are "science challenged," it doesn't take a degree in physics to operate a slow cooker. It's about the easiest machine there is on the market. It's certainly far less complicated than an espresso machine or even a waffle maker. In this chapter you'll learn about slow cookers and how to get the best results from them.

Slow cookers are inexpensive to operate; they use about as much electricity as a 60-watt bulb. They are also as easy to operate as flipping on a light switch.

Slow cookers operate by cooking food using indirect heat at a low temperature for an extended period of time. Here's the difference: Direct heat is the power of a stove burner underneath a pot, while indirect heat is the overall heat that surrounds foods as they bake in the oven.

You can purchase a slow cooker for as little as $20 at a discount store, while the top-of-the-line ones sell for more than $200. They all function in the same simple way; what increases the cost is the "bells and whistles" factors. Slow cookers come in both round and oval shapes but they operate the same regardless of shape.

Food is assembled in a pottery insert that fits inside a metal housing and is topped with a clear lid. The food cooks from the heat generated by the circular heating wires encased between the slow cooker's outer and inner layers of metal. The coils never directly touch the crockery insert. As the element heats, it gently warms the air between the two layers of metal, and it is the hot air that touches the pottery. This construction method eliminates the need for stirring because no part of the pot gets hotter than any other.

On the front of this metal casing is the control knob. All slow cookers have Low and High settings, and most also have a Stay Warm position. Some new machines have a programmable option that enables you to start food on High and then the slow cooker automatically reduces the heat to Low after a programmed time.

The largest variation in slow cookers is their size, which range from tiny 1-quart models that are excellent for hot dips and fondue but fairly useless for anything else to gigantic 7-quart models that are excellent for large families and large batches.

Most of the recipes in this book were written for and tested in a 4- or 5-quart slow cooker; that is what is meant by medium. Either of those sizes makes enough for four to eight people, depending on the recipe. In a few cases, such as for lamb shanks that take up a lot of room as they cook, a large slow cooker is specified.

Rival introduced the first slow cooker, the Crock-Pot, in 1971, and the introductory slogan remains true more than 35 years later: It "cooks all day while the cook's away." Like such trademarked names as Kleenex for paper tissue or Formica for plastic laminate, Crock-Pot has almost become synonymous with the slow cooker. However, not all slow cookers are Crock-Pots, so the generic term is used in this book.

Slow Cookers and Food Safety

Questions always arise as to the safety of slow cookers. The Food Safety and Inspection Service of the U.S. Department of Agriculture approves slow cooking as a method for safe food preparation. The lengthy cooking and the steam created within the tightly covered pot combine to destroy any bacteria that might be present in the food. But you do have to be careful.

It's far more common for foodborne illness to start with meat, poultry, and seafood than from contaminated fruits and vegetables. That is why it's not wise to cook whole chickens or cuts of meat larger than those specified in the recipes in this book because during slow cooking, these large items remain too long in the bacterial "danger zone"—between 40°F and 140°F. It is important that food reaches the higher temperature in less than two hours and remains at more than 140°F for at least 30 minutes.

If you want to cook large roasts, brown them under the oven broiler or in a skillet on top of the stove over direct heat before you place them into the slow cooker. This will help the chilled meat heat up faster as well as produce a dish that is more visually appealing. Also begin with liquid that is boiling.

Getting a jump-start on dinner while you're preparing breakfast may seem like a Herculean task, and it is possible to prep the ingredients destined for the slow cooker the night before—with some limitations. If you cut meat or vegetables in advance, store them separately in the refrigerator and layer them in the slow cooker in the morning. However, do not store the cooker insert in the refrigerator because that will also increase the amount of time it takes to heat the food to a temperature that kills bacteria.

Concern about food safety extends to after a meal is cooked and the leftovers are ready for storage. As long as the temperature remains 140°F or higher,

food will stay safe for many hours in the slow cooker. Leftovers, however, should never be refrigerated in the crockery insert because it will take them too long to go through the "danger zone" in the other direction—from hot to cold.

Freeze or refrigerate leftovers in shallow containers within two hours after a dish has finished cooking. Also, food should never be reheated in the slow cooker because it takes too long for chilled food to reheat. Bacteria are a problem on cooked food as well as raw ingredients. The slow cooker can be used to keep food warm—and without the fear of burning it—once it has been reheated on the stove or in the oven.

One of the other concerns about food safety and the slow cooker is if there is a loss of power in the house—especially if you don't know when it occurred in the cooking process. If you're home, and the amount of time was minimal, add it back into your end time. If the time without power increases to more than 30 minutes, finish the food by conventional cooking, adding more liquid, if necessary.

However, if you set the slow cooker before you left for work, and realize from electric clocks that power was off for more than an hour, it's best to discard the food, even if it looks done. You have no idea if the power outage occurred before the food passed through the "danger zone." I subscribe to the "better safe than sorry" motto.

Always thaw food before placing it in the slow cooker to ensure the trip from 40°F to 140°F is accomplished quickly and efficiently. While adding a package of frozen green beans will slow up the cooking, starting with a frozen pot roast or chicken breast will make it impossible for the low temperature of the slow cooker to accomplish this task.

Slow Cooker Hints

Slow cookers can be perplexing if you're not accustomed to using one. Here are some general tips to help you master slow cooker conundrums:

* Remember that cooking times are wide approximations—within hours rather than minutes! That's because the age or power of a slow cooker as well as the temperature of ingredients must be taken into account. Check the food at the beginning of the stated cooking time, and then gauge if it needs more time, and about how much time. If carrots or cubes of potato are still rock-hard, for example, turn the heat to High if cooking on Low, and realize that you're looking at another hour or so.
* Foods cook faster on the bottom of a slow cooker than at the top because there are more heat coils and they are totally immersed in the simmering liquid.
* Appliance manufacturers say that slow cookers can be left on either High or Low unattended, but use your own judgment. If you're going to be out of the house all day, it's advisable to cook food on Low. If, on the other hand, you're going to be gone for just a few hours, the food will be safe on High.
* Use leaf versions of dried herbs such as thyme and rosemary rather than ground versions. Ground herbs tend to lose potency during many hours in the slow cooker.
* Don't add dairy products except at the end of the cooking time, as noted in the recipes. They can curdle if cooked for too long.
* Season the dishes with pepper or crushed red pepper flakes at the end of cooking time, because these ingredients can become harsh from too many hours in the pot.

* If you want a sauce to have a more intense flavor, you can reduce the liquid in two ways. If cooking on Low, raise the heat to High, and remove the lid for the last hour of cooking. This will achieve some evaporation of the liquid. Or, remove the liquid either with a bulb baster or strain the liquid from the solids, and reduce them in a saucepan on the stove.

While in many households slow cookers are banished to the basement when screens replace storm windows during the warmer months, in my kitchen at least one lives on the counter all summer. Running the slow cooker doesn't raise the kitchen temperature by even a degree, and you can be outside enjoying the warm weather while it's cooking away.

Slow Cooker Cautions

Slow cookers are benign, but they are electrical appliances with all the concomitant hazards of any machine plugged into a live wire. Be careful that the cord is not frayed in any way, and plug the slow cooker into an outlet that is not near the sink.

Here are some tips on how to handle them:

* Never leave a slow cooker plugged in when not in use. It's all too easy to accidentally turn it on and not notice until the crockery insert cracks from overheating with nothing in it.
* Conversely, do not preheat the empty insert while you're preparing the food because the insert could crack when you add the cold food.
* Never submerge the metal casing in water, or fill it with water. While the inside of the metal does occasionally get dirty, you can clean it quite well with an abrasive cleaner, and then wipe it with a damp cloth or paper towel. While it's not aesthetically pleasing to see dirty metal, do remember that food never touches it, so if there are a few drips here and there it's not really important.
* Always remember that the insert is fragile, so don't drop it. Also, don't put a hot insert on a cold counter; that could cause it to break, too. The reverse is also true. While you can use the insert as a casserole in a conventional oven (assuming the lid is glass and not plastic), it cannot be put into a preheated oven if chilled.
* Resist the temptation to look and stir. Every time you take the lid off the slow cooker you need to add 10 minutes of cooking time if cooking on High and 20 minutes if cooking on Low to compensate. Certain recipes in this book, especially those for fish, instruct you to add ingredients during the cooking time. In those cases the heat loss from opening the pot has been factored in to the total cooking time.
* Don't add more liquid to a slow cooker recipe than that specified in the recipe. Even if the food is not submerged in liquid when you start, foods such as meats and vegetables give off liquid as they cook; in the slow cooker, that additional liquid does not evaporate.

Modern slow cookers heat slightly hotter than those made thirty years ago; the Low setting on a slow cooker is about 200°F while the High setting is close to 300°F. If you have a vintage appliance, it's a good idea to test it to make sure it still has the power to heat food sufficiently. Leave 2 quarts water at room temperature overnight, and then pour the water into the slow cooker in the morning. Heat it on Low for 8 hours. The temperature should be 185°F after 8 hours. Use an instant read thermometer to judge it. If it is lower, any food you cook in this cooker might not pass through the danger zone rapidly enough.

High-Altitude Adjustment

Rules for slow cooking, along with all other modes of cooking, change when the slow cooker is located more than 3,000 feet above sea level. At high altitudes the air is thinner so water boils at a lower temperature and comes to a boil more quickly. The rule is to always cook on High when above 3,000 feet; use the Low setting as a Keep Warm setting.

Other compensations are to reduce the liquid in a recipe by a few tablespoons, and add about 5 to 10 percent more cooking time. The liquid may be bubbling, but it's not 212°F at first.

Converting Recipes for the Slow Cooker

Once you feel comfortable with your slow cooker, you'll probably want to use it to prepare your favorite recipes you now cook on the stove or in the oven. The best recipes to convert are "wet" ones with a lot of liquid, like stews, soups, chilies, and other braised foods. Not all dishes can be easily converted to slow cooked dishes. Even if a dish calls for liquid, if it's supposed to be cooked or baked uncovered, chances are it will not be successfully transformed to a slow cooker recipe, because the food will not brown and the liquid will not evaporate.

The easiest way to convert your recipes is to find a similar one in this book and use its cooking time for guidance. When looking for a similar recipe, take into account the amount of liquid specified as well as the quantity of food. The liquid transfers the heat from the walls of the insert into the food itself, and the liquid heats in direct proportion to its measure. You should look for similar recipes as well as keep in mind some general guidelines:

* Most any stew or roast takes 8 to 12 hours on Low and 4 to 6 hours on High.
* Chicken dishes cook more rapidly. Count on 6 to 8 hours on Low and 3 to 4 hours on High.
* Quadruple the time from conventional cooking to cooking on Low, and at least double it for cooking on High.

* Cut back on the amount of liquid used in stews and other braised dishes by about half. Unlike cooking on the stove or in the oven, there is little to no evaporation in the slow cooker.

* For soups, cut back on the liquid by one third if the soup is supposed to simmer uncovered, and cut back by one fourth if the soup is simmered covered. Even when covered, a soup that is simmering on the stove has more evaporation than one cooked in the slow cooker.

Stocking Up

These stocks are referenced in countless recipes in this book. Stocks are no more difficult to make than boiling water; all they are is lots of water into which other ingredients simmer for many hours to create water with an enriched flavor.

In the same way that you can use bits of leftover vegetables in soups, many of the vegetables that go into stocks would otherwise end up in the garbage can or compost bin. Save those carrot and onion peelings, parsley stems, the base off a celery stalk, and the dark green scallion tops. All of those foods might not wend their way into cooking a dish, but they're fine for stock!

I keep different bags in my freezer in anticipation of making stock on a regular basis. There are individual ones for chicken trimmings, beef and veal (but not pork) trimmings, shrimp shells, fish skin and bones; and one for vegetables past their prime and their trimmings. When one is full, it's time to make stock.

Once your stock is cooked—and the fat removed from chicken and beef stock—you should freeze it in containers of different sizes. I do about half a batch in heavy, resealable quart bags; they are the basis for soups. Bags take up less room in the freezer than containers. Freeze them flat on a baking sheet and then they can be stacked on a freezer shelf or in the cubbyholes on the freezer door.

I then freeze stock in 1-cup measures and some in ice cube trays. Measure the capacity of your ice cube tray with a measuring tablespoon; it will be somewhere between 1 and 3 tablespoons. Keep a bag of stock cubes for those recipes that require just a small amount.

Chicken Stock

Chicken stock is used more than any other stock. It adds a rich flavor to soups not created when using water, and it is used in recipes for pork and veal as well as poultry. You'll see in the variations at the end of this recipe that there are ways to make it more appropriate to various ethnic cuisines too.

Makes 2 quarts | Prep time: 10 minutes | Minimum cook time: 4 hours in a medium slow cooker

2 quarts boiling water
2 pounds chicken pieces
(bones, skin, wing tips, etc.)
1 carrot, cut into ½-inch chunks
1 medium onion, sliced
1 celery rib, sliced
1 tablespoon black peppercorns
3 parsley sprigs, rinsed
3 thyme sprigs, rinsed, or 1 teaspoon dried
2 garlic cloves, peeled
1 bay leaf

1. Pour water into the slow cooker. Add chicken pieces, carrot, onion, celery, peppercorns, parsley, thyme, garlic, and bay leaf. Cook on Low for 8 to 10 hours or on High for 4 to 5 hours, or until chicken and vegetables are falling apart.

2. Strain stock through a sieve into a mixing bowl. Press down on solids with the back of a spoon to extract as much liquid as possible. Discard solids.

3. Chill stock. Remove and discard fat layer from top. Ladle stock into containers.

Note: The stock can be refrigerated for up to 4 days, or frozen for up to 6 months.

Variations:
* Substitute ham bones for the chicken for Ham Stock.
* Add 3 tablespoons sliced fresh ginger and 4 scallions, white parts and 4 inches of green tops, for Asian Chicken Stock.
* Substitute cilantro for the parsley, and add 1 jalapeño or serrano chile and 1 sprig fresh oregano (or 1 teaspoon dried) for Latin Chicken Stock.
* For browner chicken stock: Preheat the oven broiler, and line a broiler pan with heavy-duty aluminum foil. Broil chicken bones for 3 minutes per side, or until browned, and use the browned bones for the stock.

Starting the time in the slow cooker with the liquid already boiling saves hours of cooking time. This is a tip that can be applied to anything you cook in the slow cooker. To test to see how much time it saves, start a recipe and see how long it takes to come to a boil. That is the amount of time you can save.

Beef Stock

For a long-simmered meat dish, here's your key to delicious flavor. You'll notice that I don't add salt to any of the stocks because they can then be reduced for sauces without becoming salty. This is especially important for beef stock.

Makes 2 quarts | Prep time: 15 minutes | Minimum cook time: 5 hours in a medium slow cooker

2 pounds beef shank or meaty beef bones
2 quarts boiling water
1 carrot, cut into ½-inch chunks
1 medium onion, sliced
1 celery rib, sliced
1 tablespoon black peppercorns
3 parsley sprigs, rinsed
3 thyme sprigs, rinsed, or 1 teaspoon dried
2 garlic cloves, peeled
1 bay leaf

1. Preheat the oven broiler, and line a broiler pan with heavy-duty aluminum foil. Broil beef for 3 minutes per side or until browned. Transfer beef to the slow cooker, and pour in any juices that have collected in the pan.

2. Add water, carrot, onion, celery, peppercorns, parsley, thyme, garlic, and bay leaf. Cook on Low for 10 to 12 hours or on High for 5 to 6 hours, or until meat is very soft.

3. Strain stock through a sieve into a mixing bowl. Press down on solids with the back of a spoon to extract as much liquid as possible. Discard solids.

4. Chill stock. Remove and discard fat layer from top. Ladle stock into containers.

Note: The stock can be refrigerated for up to 4 days, or frozen for up to 6 months.

Variation:
* Substitute veal shanks or veal breast for the beef for a more delicate Veal Stock.

If you have gravy from a meat dish remaining when there's no more meat, feel free to add it to the beef stock. It will enrich the flavor.

Vegetable Stock

Even if you're cooking a vegetarian dish, it's important to start with vegetable stock rather than adding more vegetables to the dish. It creates the background for all other flavors.

Makes 2 quarts | Prep time: 10 minutes | Minimum cook time: 3 hours in a medium slow cooker

2 quarts boiling water

2 carrots, thinly sliced

2 celery ribs, sliced

2 leeks, white parts only, thinly sliced

1 small onion, thinly sliced

1 tablespoon black peppercorns

3 parsley sprigs, rinsed

3 thyme sprigs, rinsed, or 1 teaspoon dried

2 garlic cloves, peeled

1 bay leaf

1. Pour water into the slow cooker, and add carrots, celery, leeks, onion, peppercorns, parsley, thyme, garlic, and bay leaf. Cook on Low for 6 to 8 hours or on High for 3 to 4 hours, or until vegetables are soft.

2. Strain stock through a sieve into a mixing bowl. Press down on solids with the back of a spoon to extract as much liquid as possible. Discard solids.

3. Chill stock, and then ladle stock into containers.

Note: The stock can be refrigerated for up to 4 days, or frozen for up to 6 months.

Save the water you use when boiling mildly flavored vegetables such as carrots or green beans, and make them part of the liquid used for the stock. However, the water from any member of the cabbage family, like broccoli or cauliflower, is too strong.

Seafood Stock

I prefer using seafood stock to fish stock in recipes because I've found it to be more delicate. If you have a fishmonger nearby who sells cooked lobster meat, they'll either give you the shells or charge you a very modest amount for them.

Makes 2 quarts | Prep time: 10 minutes | Minimum cook time: 4 hours in a medium slow cooker

3 lobster bodies (whole lobsters from which the tail and claw meat has been removed) or 2 lobster bodies and the shells from 2 pounds raw shrimp

2 quarts boiling water

1 cup dry white wine

1 carrot, cut into ½-inch chunks

2 leeks, white parts only, sliced

1 celery rib, sliced

1 tablespoon black peppercorns

3 parsley sprigs, rinsed

3 thyme sprigs, rinsed, or 1 teaspoon dried

3 sprigs fresh tarragon, or 1 teaspoon dried

2 garlic cloves, peeled

1 bay leaf

1. Pull the top shell off the lobster body. Scrape off and discard feathery gills, then break the body into small pieces. Place pieces into the slow cooker, and repeat with remaining lobster bodies. Add shrimp shells, if used.

2. Pour boiling water and wine into the slow cooker, and add carrots, leeks, celery, peppercorns, parsley, thyme, tarragon, garlic, and bay leaf. Cook on Low for 8 to 10 hours or on High for 4 to 5 hours, or until vegetables are soft.

3. Strain stock through a sieve into a mixing bowl. Press down on solids with the back of a spoon to extract as much liquid as possible. Discard solids.

4. Chill stock, and then ladle stock into containers.

Note: The stock can be refrigerated for up to 4 days, or frozen for up to 6 months.

Variation:

* Substitute 1½ pounds fish trimmings such as skin, bones, and heads from any firm-fleshed white fish such as snapper or cod for the shellfish for Fish Stock.

> Although there are now a lot of commercial fish and seafood stocks on the market, in a pinch you can also substitute diluted bottled clam juice. Use a proportion of two-thirds clam juice to one-third water.

Chapter 2

Antipasti

Small Nibbles Before a Meal

*A*ntipasti is a term that's now used the world over for nibbles, and antipasti—literally "before the meal"—are part and parcel of meals in every region of Italy. While the majority of dishes comprising the antipasti are meats, cheeses, olives, and other foods that are purchased, some of the smaller touches are homemade, and those are the dishes you'll find in this chapter.

Most of these recipes are toppings for crostini, small slices of toast, and bruschetta, thicker and larger slices of toast. When preparing an elaborate antipasti table, I always serve crostini because the smaller amount of bread is not as filling. However, if you're just setting out a few dishes and platters, you may want the more substantial look of bruschetta. At the end of the chapter are a few other vegetable dishes and salads. I've noted which ones could also be served as a side dish.

Antipasti are great for all parties because they are served at room temperature and can be left on the table for a relatively long period of time. Hosts merely have to worry about replenishing, rather than being tied to the stove.

Crostini

Crostini (pronounced *kroh-STEEN-nee*) translates to "little toasts," and comes from the Latin word *crusta*, meaning crust. These slices, very popular in Tuscany, are usually baked, and rubbed with oil before toasting them.

Makes 20 pieces | *Prep time: 10 minutes* | *Start to finish: 20 minutes*

20 slices thin Italian bread, ½-inch thick and 2x3 inches in size

⅓ cup olive oil

1 garlic clove, halved

1. Preheat the oven to 375°F, and line a baking sheet with heavy-duty aluminum foil.

2. Brush both sides of bread slices with olive oil, and arrange bread on the prepared baking sheet. Bake until bread is beginning to brown, about 5 to 6 minutes.

3. Remove bread from the oven, and rub one side of toasts with cut surface of garlic clove.

Note: The toasts can be prepared up to 2 days in advance and kept at room temperature in an airtight container.

Variation:

✳ Substitute melted unsalted butter for the olive oil.

While making the toasts in advance is a great boon for home cooks without the number of hands available to do the job in a restaurant kitchen, you really want to make sure they're not soggy. If it's been humid, and your toasts are less than crisp, reheat them in a 350°F oven for 3 to 4 minutes.

Bruschetta

Bruschetta (pronounced *broo-SKEH-tah*) are like the rustic cousins to crostini. These toasts are thicker in width, larger in diameter, and are toasted on a grill rather than in the oven. Bruschetta dates back to the fifteenth century.

Makes 6 to 8 | *Prep time: 10 minutes* | *Start to finish: 20 minutes*

6 to 8 slices rustic Italian bread, ¾-inch thick and 3x4 inches in size

¼ cup olive oil

1 garlic clove, halved

1. Light a charcoal or gas grill, or preheat the oven broiler.

2. Grill or broil bread for 1 to 2 minutes per side, or until brown. Brush both sides of toasts with olive oil, and rub one side of toasts with cut surface of garlic clove.

Note: The toasts should not be prepared more than 2 hours in advance.

Variation:

∗ Substitute melted butter for the olive oil, and sprinkle toasts lightly with freshly grated Parmesan cheese in addition to rubbing them with garlic.

There are two species of garlic grown in Italy that have been given Protected Geographical Status by the European Union. *Aglio Bianco Polesano* comes from the Veneto, and *Aglio di Voghiera* is native to Ferrara in Emilia-Romagna.

Roasted Tomato Topping for Crostini or Bruschetta

It could be considered a "food crime" to top toasts with anything except raw tomatoes during the summer, but come winter small plum tomatoes are about the best option, and they are really enhanced by being cooked this way. I also serve them as a garnish for roasted meats.

Makes 1¹/₂ cups | Prep time: 10 minutes | Minimum cook time: 1¹/₂ hours in a medium slow cooker

6 ripe plum tomatoes, cored, cut in half lengthwise, and seeded

4 garlic cloves, unpeeled

2 tablespoons olive oil

1 teaspoon fresh thyme or pinch dried

¹/₂ teaspoon granulated sugar

Salt and freshly ground black pepper to taste

¹/₂ cup firmly packed basil leaves

1. Pour ¹/₄ cup water into the slow cooker, and arrange tomatoes and garlic cloves in one layer. Drizzle olive oil over all. Combine thyme, sugar, salt, and pepper in a small bowl, and sprinkle over tomatoes.

2. Cook on Low for 3 to 4 hours or on High for 1¹/₂ to 2 hours, or until tomatoes are very tender. Remove tomatoes and garlic from the slow cooker with a slotted spoon, and reserve liquid in the slow cooker.

3. When cool enough to handle, peel garlic and mash it into a paste. Combine mashed garlic with a few tablespoons reserved tomato liquid. To serve, spread paste on crostini or bruschetta, top with tomato half and a basil leaf. Serve warm or at room temperature.

Note: The tomatoes and paste can be prepared up to 2 days in advance and refrigerated, tightly covered. Bring them to room temperature before assembling.

Variation:

✽ Substitute 1 tablespoon chopped fresh basil or oregano for the thyme, and substitute red pepper flakes for the black pepper.

Drizzle is a fancy term for pouring a small amount of liquid slowly over a large area rather than pouring it all in one place. You can drizzle with a measuring cup, but the liquid is more likely to scatter over more territory if you use a spoon.

Spicy Kale Topping for Crostini or Bruschetta

Kale is the renegade cousin of the cabbage family. Its flavor is very mild, and it has frilly deep green leaves that look like a bouquet of flowers rather than a tight head. This topping adds a deep green hue to your antipasti options.

Makes 1¹/₂ cups | Prep time: 15 minutes | Minimum cook time: 2 hours in a medium slow cooker

1½ pounds kale

¼ cup olive oil

4 garlic cloves, minced

½ to ¾ teaspoon crushed red pepper flakes

¾ cup Vegetable Stock (page 23), Chicken Stock (page 19), or purchased stock

Salt to taste

1. Rinse kale, and discard thick ribs and stems. Cut kale into ¹/₂-inch slices.

2. Heat oil in a deep saucepan over medium-high heat. Add garlic and crushed red pepper flakes, and cook for 30 seconds, stirring constantly. Add kale a few handfuls at a time, and stir. Cover the pan for 30 seconds, and then stir again. Continue until all kale is wilted. Scrape kale into the slow cooker.

3. Add stock to the slow cooker, and stir well. Cook on Low for 3 to 4 hours or on High for 1¹/₂ to 2 hours, or until kale is almost tender. If cooking on Low, raise the heat to High. Cook kale uncovered for an additional 30 to 45 minutes, or until very tender. Season to taste with salt.

4. To serve, remove kale from the slow cooker with a slotted spoon, and mound on toasts. Serve warm or at room temperature.

Note: The dish can be prepared up to 2 days in advance and refrigerated, tightly covered. Reheat it, covered, over low heat until warm, stirring occasionally.

Variation:
✳ Substitute Swiss chard or collard greens for the kale.

The easiest way to break apart a whole head of garlic is to slam the root end onto the countertop. It should then separate easily.

White Bean Topping for Crostini or Bruschetta

Beans of all types are a traditional topping, and the roasted red pepper and green parsley make this version as colorful as the Italian flag.

Makes 2¹/₂ cups | Prep time: 15 minutes | Minimum cook time: 2¹/₂ hours in a medium slow cooker

1 cup dried navy beans

2 teaspoons salt

¹/₃ cup extra-virgin olive oil

¹/₄ cup freshly squeezed lemon juice

2 garlic cloves, minced

1 roasted red bell pepper, cut into ¹/₂-inch dice (optional)

¹/₂ cup chopped fresh parsley

1 tablespoon fresh thyme or ¹/₂ teaspoon dried

Salt and freshly ground black pepper to taste

1. Rinse beans in a colander and place them in a mixing bowl covered with 1 quart cold water and salt. Allow beans to soak for at least six hours, or overnight. Or place beans into a saucepan with water and salt, and bring to a boil over high heat. Boil 1 minute. Turn off the heat, cover the pan, and soak beans for 1 hour. With either soaking method, drain beans, discard soaking water, and begin cooking as soon as possible.

2. Place drained beans in the slow cooker, and add enough water to cover them by 2 inches. Cook on Low for 5 to 7 hours or on High for 2¹/₂ to 3 hours, or until beans are cooked but still al dente. Drain beans, and reserve ¹/₂ cup of cooking liquid.

3. Combine ¹/₂ cup of beans, oil, lemon juice, and garlic in a food processor fitted with a steel blade or in a blender. Puree until smooth, and stir puree back in to remaining beans. Add red pepper (if using), parsley, and thyme, and stir gently. Add as much reserved cooking liquid as needed to make mixture moist, and season to taste with salt and pepper.

4. To serve, mound mixture on top of toasts. Serve warm or at room temperature.

Note: The dish can be prepared up to 2 days in advance and refrigerated, tightly covered. Reheat it, covered, over low heat until warm, stirring occasionally.

Variations:

✳ Substitute garbanzo beans for the white beans, and add ¹/₂ cup chopped prosciutto.

✳ Add 1 to 2 (5-ounce) cans Italian tuna packed in olive oil to the beans, and use the oil from the cans in place of the oil in the recipe.

> Beans are high in carbohydrates, which makes them a natural thickener for dishes. That's the purpose of mashing some of the beans for this dish, and the same procedure can be used when cooking any bean dish.

Bell Pepper Topping for Crostini or Bruschetta

Peperonata (pronounced *peh-peh-roh-NAH-tah*) is a colorful and flavorful dish that can be served as a topping for toasts or as a part of the antipasti presentation on its own.

Makes 1¹/₂ cups | Prep time: 20 minutes | Minimum cook time: 2 hours in a medium slow cooker

⅓ cup olive oil

2 large onions, halved and thinly sliced

1 large green bell pepper, seeds and ribs removed, and thinly sliced

1 large red bell pepper, seeds and ribs removed, and thinly sliced

1 large orange or yellow bell pepper, seeds and ribs removed, and thinly sliced

2 garlic cloves, minced (optional)

2 ripe plum tomatoes, cored, seeded, and diced

3 tablespoons Vegetable Stock (page 23), Chicken Stock (page 19), or purchased stock

2 tablespoons chopped fresh rosemary or 2 teaspoons dried

1 to 2 tablespoons balsamic vinegar

Salt and freshly ground black pepper to taste

1. Heat oil in a large skillet over medium-high heat. Add onions, green bell pepper, red bell pepper, and orange bell pepper, and garlic, if using. Cook, stirring frequently, for 3 minutes, or until onions are translucent. Scrape mixture into the slow cooker.

2. Add tomatoes, stock, and rosemary to the slow cooker, and stir well. Cook on Low for 4 to 5 hours or on High for 2 to 2¹/₂ hours, or until peppers are very tender. Stir in vinegar, and season to taste with salt and pepper.

3. To serve, mound mixture on top of toasts. Serve warm or at room temperature.

Note: The dish can be prepared up to 2 days in advance and refrigerated, tightly covered. Reheat it, covered, over low heat until warm, stirring occasionally.

Variations:

* Add 2 tablespoons small capers, drained and rinsed, to the slow cooker.
* Add 2 to 3 finely chopped anchovy fillets to the slow cooker, and omit the salt.
* Add ¹/₄ cup chopped raisins to the slow cooker.

It's easier to slice and dice bell peppers from the inside out. Once the seeds and ribs have been removed, place the shiny, slippery skin on your cutting board, and you'll find it's easier to control your knife and cut the size pieces you desire.

Chicken Liver Topping for Crostini or Bruschetta

Livers of many animals play a role in Italian cuisine, and chicken livers on top of toasts is traditional in many regions. These are cooked with a reduction of sweet vermouth and punctuated with salty capers.

Makes 3 cups | Prep time: 15 minutes | Minimum cook time: 2 hours in a medium slow cooker

1½ pounds chicken livers

4 tablespoons (½ stick) unsalted butter

2 tablespoons olive oil

1 small red onion, chopped

2 garlic cloves, minced (optional)

1 cup sweet red vermouth

3 tablespoons capers

½ cup chopped fresh parsley

Salt and freshly ground black pepper to taste

Lemon wedges for serving

1. Rinse chicken livers, and pat dry on paper towels. Trim chicken livers of all fat, and discard veins connecting the two lobes. Cut livers into ¹/₂-inch pieces, and set aside.

2. Heat butter and oil in a skillet over medium-high heat. Add onion and garlic, if using, and cook, stirring frequently, for 3 minutes, or until onion is translucent. Pour vermouth into the skillet, and cook over high heat until liquid is reduced by two-thirds. Scrape mixture into the slow cooker.

3. Add livers and capers to the slow cooker, and stir gently. Cook on Low for 3 to 4 hours or on High for 1¹/₂ to 2 hours, or until livers are cooked through. Allow mixture to cool for 15 minutes, then stir in parsley, and season to taste with salt and pepper.

4. To serve, mound topping onto toasts, and squeeze a few drops of lemon juice over each toast. Serve warm or at room temperature.

Note: The dish can be prepared up to 2 days in advance without the parsley and refrigerated, tightly covered. Reheat it, covered, over low heat until warm, stirring occasionally, then stir in the parsley.

Variation:
* Substitute chopped brine-cured green olives for the capers.

Many cookbooks call for soaking chicken livers in milk for at least a few hours, if not overnight, and then discarding the milk. They claim that the soaking removes the gamey flavor from chicken livers, so if you find that offensive, try the soak.

Red Onion Topping for Crostini or Bruschetta

The innate sweetness of red onions is enhanced by balsamic vinegar and contrasted with the smoky note of pancetta in this colorful topping. This freezes very well, so keep some on hand for instant entertaining.

Makes 1¹/₂ cups | Prep time: 20 minutes | Minimum cook time: 3 hours in a medium slow cooker

3 tablespoons olive oil

¹/₂ cup finely chopped pancetta

3 large red onions, halved and thinly sliced

2 garlic cloves, minced

Salt and freshly ground black pepper to taste

1 tablespoon freshly squeezed lemon juice

1 teaspoon fennel seeds, crushed

1 tablespoon balsamic vinegar

1. Heat oil in a large skillet over medium-high heat. Add pancetta, and cook for 4 to 5 minutes, or until lightly browned. Add onions and garlic to the skillet, toss to coat well, and season to taste with salt and pepper. Reduce the heat to low, cover the skillet and cook for 10 minutes. Scrape onion mixture into the slow cooker, and add lemon juice and fennel seed.

2. Cook on High for 1 hour, remove the cover, and stir onions. Cook for an additional 2 to 3 hours, or until onions are very tender. Sprinkle with vinegar, and season to taste with salt and pepper. To serve, mound mixture on top of toasts. Serve warm or at room temperature.

Note: The dish can be prepared up to 2 days in advance and refrigerated, tightly covered. Reheat it, covered, over low heat until warm, stirring occasionally.

Variation:
* Substitute 2 anchovy fillets, finely chopped, for salt.

> Adding salt to onions makes them soften faster because the salt draws out the natural moisture, and the addition of sugar helps in the browning process.

White Bean and Tuna Salad

Italians eat a lot of canned tuna, and with good reason. Italian tuna packed in olive oil has a wonderful flavor and texture. In this dish it's mixed with beans and scallions in a lemony dressing.

Makes 8 to 10 servings as part of an antipasti table or 4 to 6 servings as a side dish | Prep time: 15 minutes | Minimum cook time: 2 hours in a medium slow cooker plus at least 2 hours to chill

2 cups dried white navy beans

2 teaspoons salt

2 garlic cloves, minced (optional)

⅓ cup chopped fresh parsley

4 scallions, white parts and 2 inches of green tops, chopped

3 tablespoons freshly squeezed lemon juice

Freshly ground black pepper to taste

2 (5-ounce) cans Italian tuna packed in olive oil, drained with oil reserved

1. Rinse beans in a colander and place them in a mixing bowl covered with 1 quart cold water and salt. Allow beans to soak for at least six hours, or overnight. Or place beans into a saucepan with water and salt, and bring to a boil over high heat. Boil 1 minute. Turn off the heat, cover the pan, and soak beans for 1 hour. With either soaking method, drain beans, discard soaking water, and begin cooking as soon as possible.

2. Place drained beans in the slow cooker, and add enough water to cover them by 2 inches and garlic, if using. Cook on Low for 4 to 6 hours or on High for 2 to 3 hours, or until beans are tender. Drain beans and chill them well.

3. Combine parsley and scallions in a mixing bowl, and stir in reserved oil from the canned tuna, lemon juice, salt, and pepper. Add chilled beans and stir well. Gently fold in tuna, breaking it up into chunks.

Note: The dish can be prepared up to 2 days in advance and refrigerated, tightly covered. Allow it to sit out for 30 minutes before serving if chilled.

Variations:

✳ Substitute ¹/₂ pound cooked baby shrimp or lump crabmeat for the tuna, and add ¹/₄ cup olive oil to the dressing.

✳ Omit the tuna and add ¹/₄ cup olive oil to the dressing.

Traditional Hawaiian cooks add a few slices of ginger to the water in which dried beans are cooking as a way to alleviate the potential gas problem. The ginger is not detectable in the finished dish.

Garbanzo Bean Salad

This is one of the prettiest salads you can serve as part of an antipasti table, and it's delicious too. The nutty flavor of the beans is a wonderful contrast to the colorful and bitter chopped radicchio.

Makes 8 to 10 servings as part of an antipasti table or 4 to 6 servings as a side dish | Prep time: 20 minutes | Minimum cook time: 3 hours in a medium slow cooker plus at least 2 hours to chill

1 cup dried garbanzo beans

2 teaspoons salt

4 garlic cloves, minced, divided

1 bay leaf

¼ cup red wine vinegar

¼ cup freshly squeezed orange juice

3 tablespoons chopped fresh parsley

1 tablespoon chopped fresh rosemary or 1 teaspoon dried

2 teaspoons fresh thyme or ½ teaspoon dried

2 teaspoons chopped fresh oregano or ½ teaspoon dried

1 teaspoon grated orange zest

⅓ cup olive oil

¾ cup pitted oil-cured black olives, chopped

½ small red onion, diced

1 small head radicchio, rinsed, cored, and chopped (optional)

Salt and freshly ground black pepper to taste

1. Rinse beans in a colander and place them in a mixing bowl covered with 1 quart cold water and salt. Allow beans to soak for at least six hours, or overnight. Or place beans into a saucepan with water and salt, and bring to a boil over high heat. Boil 1 minute. Turn off the heat, cover the pan, and soak beans for 1 hour. With either soaking method, drain beans, discard soaking water, and begin cooking as soon as possible.

2. Place drained beans in the slow cooker, and add 2 garlic cloves, bay leaf, and enough water to cover them by 2 inches. Cook on Low for 6 to 8 hours or on High for 3 to 4 hours, or until beans are cooked but still al dente. Drain beans, and chill for at least 2 hours.

3. Combine vinegar, orange juice, parsley, rosemary, thyme, oregano, and orange zest in a jar with a tight-fitting lid. Shake well. Add olive oil, and shake well again.

4. Add olives, onion, and radicchio (if using) to the bowl with beans. Toss with dressing, and season to taste with salt and pepper. Serve immediately.

Note: The beans can be cooked up to 2 days in advance and refrigerated, tightly covered. Do not assemble the salad until just prior to serving.

Variation:
* Substitute kidney beans for the garbanzo beans and Belgian endive for the radicchio.

> Salt and pepper are usually added to a salad dressing along with other seasonings. But when a dish contains a food like olives that are already salty it's best to try the salad to see if additional salt is necessary.

Roasted Garlic

Roasted garlic is a vegetable that freezes very well, so fill up the slow cooker and make a large batch. I add it to everything from mashed potatoes to scrambled eggs. Serve these heads whole, with some crostini on the side for spreading with the soft and sweet cloves.

Makes 8 heads | Prep time: 10 minutes | Minimum cook time: 3 hours in a medium slow cooker

8 heads garlic

1 cup olive oil

1 tablespoon fresh thyme
or ½ teaspoon dried

Salt and freshly ground black pepper
to taste

1. Cut off the top 1-inch of each garlic head to expose the cloves; reserve cut off clove portions for another use. Place heads in the slow cooker, and pour oil over them. Sprinkle with thyme, salt, and pepper.

2. Cook on High for 3 to 4 hours, or until garlic is very tender when pierced with the tip of a paring knife. Turn off the slow cooker, remove the cover, and allow garlic to cool in oil.

3. Remove garlic from oil with a slotted spoon. Pop cloves out of heads and discard skins. Transfer garlic to a storage container or heavy resealable plastic bag.

Note: The garlic can be refrigerated for up to 5 days or frozen for up to 3 months.

Variation:
* Substitute oregano or sage for the thyme.

As garlic ages, bitter green shoots begin to emerge from the individual cloves. Never buy a head if the shoots are visible, and for a recipe like this one don't use heads if you see green shoots after cutting off the top of the head. You don't have to discard the heads; break them into individual cloves and remove the green centers before chopping or mincing.

Cranberry Bean Topping for Crostini or Bruschetta

This is one of the heartier toppings in the Italian repertoire. It combines meaty beans with aromatic fennel and tomatoes, and it's topped with a sprinkling of salty prosciutto and bright green basil.

Makes 2 cups | Prep time: 20 minutes | Minimum cook time: 4^1/$_2$ hours in a medium slow cooker

¾ cup dried cranberry beans or borlotti beans

2 teaspoons salt

1 tablespoon olive oil

¼ pound pancetta, coarsely chopped

1 medium onion, diced

1 small fennel bulb, trimmed, cored, and diced

2 garlic cloves, minced

½ cup dry white wine

1 (14.5-ounce) petite diced tomatoes, drained

¾ cup Chicken Stock (page 19) or purchased stock

1 bay leaf

Freshly ground black pepper to taste

¾ cup finely diced prosciutto di Parma

3 tablespoons chopped fresh basil

1. Rinse beans in a colander and place them in a mixing bowl covered with 1 quart cold water and salt. Allow beans to soak for at least six hours, or overnight. Or place beans into a saucepan with water and salt, and bring to a boil over high heat. Boil 1 minute. Turn off the heat, cover the pan, and soak beans for 1 hour. With either soaking method, drain beans, discard soaking water, and begin cooking as soon as possible.

2. Place drained beans in the slow cooker, and add enough water to cover them by 2 inches. Cook on Low for 5 to 7 hours or on High for 2½ to 3 hours, or until beans are cooked but still al dente. Drain beans, and return them to the slow cooker.

3. While beans cook, heat oil in a medium skillet over medium-high heat. Cook pancetta for 4 to 5 minutes, or until brown. Add onion, fennel, and garlic, and cook, stirring frequently, for 3 minutes, or until onion is translucent. Add wine, and cook until wine is reduced by half. Scrape mixture into the slow cooker with the beans.

4. Add tomatoes, stock, and bay leaf to the slow cooker, and stir well. Cook on Low for 4 to 5 hours or on High for 2 to 2½ hours, or until vegetables and beans are tender. Remove and discard bay leaf, and season to taste with salt and pepper.

5. To serve, mound bean topping on top of toasts, and sprinkle with prosciutto and basil. Serve warm or at room temperature.

Note: The dish can be prepared up to 2 days in advance and refrigerated, tightly covered. Reheat it, covered, over low heat until just warm, stirring occasionally.

Variation:

* Substitute 1 (15-ounce) can cannellini or kidney beans for the dried beans. Steps 1 and 2 can be omitted, and the total cooking time is reduced to 2 hours.

> When you're instructed to drain a can of tomatoes, always save that juice. You can add it to the pot when making stocks, soups, or stews. It adds flavor, and it's free.

Braised Baby Artichokes with Prosciutto and Parmesan

It's only been in this century that it's become easy to find baby artichokes in North American markets. These small versions of the globe artichokes are totally edible; it's not necessary to remove and discard the hairy "choke." Artichokes are traditionally part of an antipasti spread.

Makes 8 to 10 servings as part of an antipasti table or 4 to 6 servings as a side dish | Prep time: 30 minutes | Minimum cook time: 3 hours in a medium slow cooker

2 lemons
2 dozen baby artichokes
3 tablespoons olive oil
3 shallots, diced
2 garlic cloves, minced
½ cup chopped prosciutto di Parma
¾ Chicken Stock (page 19) or purchased stock
½ cup dry white wine
2 tablespoons freshly squeezed lemon juice
1 tablespoon fresh thyme or ½ teaspoon dried
1 bay leaf
2 tablespoons unsalted butter
Salt and freshly ground black pepper to taste
½ cup freshly grated Parmesan cheese
2 tablespoons chopped fresh parsley

1. Place 6 cups of very cold tap water in a mixing bowl, squeeze in juice from lemons, and add lemon halves.

2. Work on 1 artichoke at a time because they discolor very quickly. If there is a stem, trim and peel the dark green skin from the stem. Break off all the small dark leaves on the bottom so that the artichoke resembles a rose bud. Cut off the top 1 inch, and then cut them in half lengthwise. Place in the lemon water, and repeat until all artichokes are trimmed.

3. Heat oil in a large skillet over medium-high heat. Add shallots, garlic, and prosciutto, and cook, stirring frequently, for 3 minutes, or until shallots are translucent. Drain artichokes and add them to the skillet along with stock, wine, lemon juice, thyme, and bay leaf. Bring to a boil, and transfer mixture to the slow cooker.

4. Cook on Low for 3 to 4 hours or on High for 1½ to 2 hours, or until artichokes are very tender. Add butter to the slow cooker, and cook until melted.

5. Remove and discard bay leaf. Season with salt and pepper to taste, and transfer artichokes and ½ cup of braising liquid to a serving dish. Combine cheese and parsley in a small bowl, and sprinkle over artichokes. Serve warm or at room temperature.

Note: The dish can be prepared up to 2 days in advance without the parsley and cheese and refrigerated, tightly covered. Reheat it, covered, over low heat until warm, stirring occasionally, then sprinkle with the topping mixture.

Variations:
* Omit the cheese and sprinkle the artichokes with ⅓ cup toasted pine nuts.
* Add 2 finely chopped anchovy fillets to the skillet, and omit the salt.

To get the maximum amount of juice from citrus fruits, roll them back and forth on a counter or prick the skin and microwave them on high power for 30 seconds.

Caponata

Caponata is a Sicilian vegetable dish that always has eggplant although some of the other ingredients can vary. The name probably comes from the Latin word *caupo,* or "tavern," because this is the sort of robust food that men would eat in taverns.

Makes 8 to 10 servings as part of an antipasti table or 4 to 6 servings as a side dish | Prep time: 25 minutes | Minimum cook time: 2½ hours in a medium slow cooker

1 (1-pound) eggplant

Salt

⅓ cup olive oil, divided

2 celery ribs, diced

1 large onion, diced

3 garlic cloves, minced

¼ cup red wine vinegar

1 teaspoon granulated sugar

1 (14.5-ounce) can diced tomatoes, undrained

1 tablespoon tomato paste

¼ cup sliced black olives

2 tablespoons small capers, drained and rinsed

2 tablespoons anchovy paste

Freshly ground black pepper to taste

1. Rinse and trim eggplant, and cut into ¾-inch cubes. Put eggplant in a colander, and sprinkle it liberally with salt. Place a plate on top of eggplant cubes, and weight the plate with cans. Place the colander in the sink or on a plate, and allow eggplant to drain for 30 minutes. Rinse eggplant cubes, and squeeze hard to remove water. Wring out remaining water with a cloth tea towel.

2. Heat half of oil in a medium skillet over medium-high heat. Add celery, onion, and garlic, and cook, stirring frequently, for 3 minutes, or until onion is translucent. Remove vegetables from the pan with a slotted spoon, and transfer them to the slow cooker.

3. Pour remaining oil into the skillet, and add eggplant cubes. Cook, stirring frequently, for 5 minutes or until eggplant is lightly browned. Spoon eggplant into the slow cooker.

4. Add vinegar, sugar, tomatoes, tomato paste, olives, capers, and anchovy paste, and stir well. Cook on Low for 5 to 6 hours or on High for 2½ to 3 hours, or until vegetables are soft. Season to taste with salt and pepper. Allow mixture to reach room temperature and serve either at room temperature or chilled.

Note: The dish can be prepared up to 2 days in advance and refrigerated, tightly covered. Allow it to sit out for 30 minutes before serving if chilled.

Variations:

✳ Add ½ cup raisins to the slow cooker.

✳ Omit the anchovy paste, and add salt at the end of the cooking time.

Capers are the flower bud of a low bush native to the Mediterranean. After harvest they're sun-dried and pickled in vinegar. Although they're customarily packed in brine, you can also find them packed in coarse salt. However you buy them, rinse them well before using.

Giardiniera Vegetables

This mélange of crisp and colorful vegetables, pronounced *jar-din-YAIR-ah,* always includes cauliflower and it's part of many antipasti tables. But usually it comes from a market. Once you see how easy it is to make, you'll always include some in your planning.

Makes 8 to 10 servings as part of an antipasti table or 4 to 6 servings as a side dish | Prep time: 15 minutes | Minimum cook time: 1½ hours in a medium slow cooker

2 carrots, thickly sliced

½ head cauliflower, broken into florets

2 broccoli crowns, broken into florets

¼ pound mixed brine-cured olives

¼ cup freshly squeezed lemon juice

1 teaspoon dried oregano

¼ teaspoon crushed red pepper flakes

Salt to taste

½ cup olive oil

1. Place a steamer basket in the slow cooker, and layer the vegetables with the carrots on the bottom, then the cauliflower and broccoli. Add ½ cup water to the slow cooker, and cook vegetables on Low for 3 to 5 hours or on High for 1½ to 2 hours, or until vegetables are crisp-tender. Plunge vegetables into a bowl of ice water to stop the cooking action and set the color. Then drain, and place them in a mixing bowl with olives.

2. Combine lemon juice, oregano, red pepper flakes, and salt in a jar with a tight-fitting lid, and shake well. Add olive oil, and shake well again.

3. Toss dressing with vegetables, and allow mixture to sit for 15 minutes before serving, tossing vegetables occasionally. Serve at room temperature.

Note: The vegetables and dressing can both be prepared up to 2 days in advance and refrigerated, tightly covered. Allow both to reach room temperature before tossing and serving.

Variations:

✳ Add 3 to 4 sun-dried tomatoes packed in olive oil, finely chopped, to the dressing.

✳ Substitute baby artichokes, halved and rubbed with lemon juice to prevent discoloration, for the broccoli.

> Steaming preserves more of the vegetables' natural nutrients than boiling. The vitamins and minerals are leached out into the hot water when you throw your veggies into boiling water.

Chapter 3

Minestre

Soups and Other Primi

oups are very popular as *primi,* or first course, in all Italian regions, and they are natural dishes to cook in the slow cooker because the best soups are those that are slowly simmered over hours to blend the flavors and showcase the various ingredients. And that's what the slow cooker does best.

You'll find a range of small soups in this chapter. Most of them feature some sort of meat, especially sausage and other cured pork products such as pancetta and prosciutto as accent flavors. However, these can be transformed into vegetarian soups by omitting the meat and substituting vegetable stock for the chicken stock specified. There are also a number of fish and seafood stews in Chapter 5 that can be served as primi in smaller portions, and all appropriate recipes have been annotated with the number of servings.

At the end of this chapter are a few other small dishes, including some wonderful Italian omelets, called frittata, which can be served hot, at room temperature, or chilled. These are similar to the tortillas served in Spanish tapas bars, and the slow cooker makes them beautifully because the gentle heat does not toughen the eggs.

Vegetable Soup with Herb Oil

What makes this soup so special is the contrast between the mellow, long-simmered flavors of the soup and the freshness of the herb oil.

Makes 4 to 6 servings | Active time: 25 minutes | Minimum cook time: 3 ¼ hours in a medium slow cooker

SOUP

3 tablespoons olive oil

1 large onion, diced

2 garlic cloves, minced

1 large carrot, sliced

½ fennel bulb, cored and diced

2 cups firmly packed thinly sliced green cabbage

5 cups Vegetable Stock (page 23) or purchased stock

1 (14.5-ounce) can diced tomatoes, undrained

2 tablespoons tomato paste

2 tablespoons chopped fresh parsley

1 tablespoon chopped fresh oregano or 1 teaspoon dried

1 tablespoon fresh thyme or ½ teaspoon dried

1 bay leaf

1 medium zucchini, diced

1 medium yellow squash, diced

1 (15-ounce) can garbanzo beans, drained and rinsed

½ cup freshly grated Parmesan cheese

¼ pound small pasta such as shells, cooked according to package directions until al dente

Salt and freshly ground black pepper to taste

HERB OIL

¾ cup firmly packed parsley leaves

2 garlic cloves, minced

2 tablespoons chopped fresh basil or 2 teaspoons dried

1 tablespoon chopped fresh rosemary or 1 teaspoon dried

½ cup olive oil

Salt and freshly ground black pepper to taste

1. Heat oil in a large skillet over medium-high heat. Add onion, garlic, carrot, fennel, and cabbage. Cook, stirring frequently, for 3 minutes, or until onion is translucent. Scrape mixture into the slow cooker.

2. Add stock, tomatoes, tomato paste, parsley, oregano, thyme, and bay leaf to the slow cooker, and stir well. Cook on Low for 4 to 6 hours or on High for 2 to 3 hours, or until vegetables are almost tender. Add zucchini and yellow squash, and cook on Low for 2 to 3 hours or on High for 1 to 2 hours, or until vegetables are tender.

3. If cooking on Low, raise the heat to High. Add beans and Parmesan to the slow cooker, and cook for 20 to 30 minutes, or until simmering. Remove and discard bay leaf, add pasta, and season to taste with salt and pepper.

4. While soup simmers, prepare herb oil. Combine parsley, garlic, basil, rosemary, and oil in a food processor fitted with the steel blade or in a blender. Puree until smooth. Season to taste with salt and pepper, and scrape mixture into a bowl.

5. To serve, ladle soup into bowls, and pass herb oil separately.

Note: The soup can be prepared up to 3 days in advance and refrigerated, tightly covered. Reheat it, covered, over low heat, stirring occasionally.

Variation:

✳ Substitute chicken stock for the vegetable stock, and add ½ pound boneless, skinless chicken, cut into ¾-inch cubes, at the onset of the cooking time.

> When soups are made with pasta, the cooked pasta should be added just prior to serving. Otherwise it will absorb stock from the soup and get mushy.

Garbanzo Bean Soup

This spicy soup is made with canned beans, so that the cooking time is far shorter than if the beans started dry and had to be soaked and cooked. It's a simple soup that allows the nutty flavor of the beans to emerge.

Makes 6 to 8 servings | Prep time: 15 minutes | Minimum cook time: 3 hours in a medium slow cooker

3 tablespoons olive oil

1 large onion, diced

1 celery rib, chopped

3 garlic cloves, minced

3 cups Vegetable Stock (page 23) or purchased stock

1 (14.5-ounce) can petite diced tomatoes, undrained

2 (15-ounce) cans garbanzo beans, drained and rinsed

2 tablespoons chopped fresh rosemary or 2 teaspoons dried

Salt and crushed red pepper flakes to taste

Freshly grated Parmesan cheese

1. Heat olive oil in a medium skillet over medium-high heat. Add onion, celery, and garlic. Cook, stirring frequently, for 3 minutes, or until onion is translucent. Scrape mixture into the slow cooker.

2. Add stock, tomatoes, garbanzo beans, and rosemary to the slow cooker, and stir well. Cook on Low for 6 to 8 hours or on High for 3 to 4 hours, or until vegetables are tender. Season to taste with salt and red pepper flakes, and serve hot, passing Parmesan cheese separately.

Note: The soup can be prepared up to 3 days in advance and refrigerated, tightly covered. Reheat it, covered, over low heat, stirring occasionally.

Variation:
✱ Substitute white beans for the garbanzo beans.

Garbanzo beans have been part of Mediterranean cuisines since the Bronze Age. In classical Greece they were a staple, and the Roman gourmet Apicius gives several recipes for them. We also know that the Roman armies traveled with them; they have been found at forts in Germany and France.

Creamy Leek and Potato Soup

The combination of leeks, potatoes, and cream is part of most European cuisines, including Italian. It's traditionally served a little lumpy, but I've also given directions for a more elegant pureed version.

Makes 6 to 8 servings | Prep time: 20 minutes | Minimum cook time: 2^1/$_4$ hours in a medium slow cooker

5 leeks, white parts only

2 tablespoons unsalted butter

2 large boiling potatoes (about 1½ pounds), peeled and cut into ¾-inch dice

4 cups Vegetable Stock (page 23), Chicken Stock (page 19), or purchased stock

¾ cup heavy whipping cream

Salt and freshly ground black pepper to taste

½ cup snipped fresh chives

1. Trim leeks, split lengthwise, and slice thinly. Place slices in a colander and rinse well under cold running water, rubbing with your fingers to dislodge all dirt. Shake leeks in the colander. Melt butter in a medium saucepan over medium heat. Add leeks, and toss with butter. Cover the pan, reduce the heat to low, and cook for 10 minutes. Scrape mixture into the slow cooker.

2. Add potatoes and stock to the slow cooker, and stir well. Cook on Low for 4½ to 6 hours or on High for 2 to 3 hours, or until potatoes are tender. If cooking on Low, raise the heat to High. Add cream, and cook soup for an additional 10 to 20 minutes, or until simmering.

3. Mash some of vegetables with a potato masher until desired consistency; the more that is mashed the thicker the soup will be. For a pureed soup, allow soup to cool for 10 minutes. Either puree it with an immersion blender, or strain solids from soup and puree them in a food processor fitted with the steel blade or in a blender. Season to taste with salt and pepper, and serve hot, sprinkling each serving with chives.

Note: The soup can be prepared up to 3 days in advance and refrigerated, tightly covered. Reheat it, covered, over low heat, stirring occasionally.

Variations:

* Add 4 to 6 cloves sliced garlic, and cook the garlic along with the leeks.

* Puree the soup, refrigerate until cold, and serve chilled.

Unlike most herbs, which should be minced with a knife, chives are best treated with a sharp pair of scissors, making small snips to get even pieces. If you don't have access to fresh chives, the best substitute for both flavor and appearance is scallion tops.

Tomato and Bread Stew

Called *Pappa al Pomodoro* in Italian, this is a rich and creamy stew flavored with fresh basil and two cheeses. It's similar to a bread pudding, but looser because it doesn't contain any eggs.

Makes 6 to 8 servings | *Prep time: 20 minutes* | *Minimum cook time: 2 hours in a medium slow cooker*

3 pounds ripe plum tomatoes

1 (1-pound) loaf Italian or French bread

¼ cup olive oil

1 large onion, chopped

2 garlic cloves, chopped

3 to 4 cups whole milk

½ cup firmly packed chopped fresh basil

½ cup grated whole milk mozzarella cheese

½ cup freshly grated Parmesan cheese

Salt and freshly ground black pepper to taste

Fresh basil leaves for garnish

Vegetable oil spray

1. Grease a slow cooker liberally with vegetable oil spray. Rinse tomatoes and discard core. Cut tomatoes in half and squeeze over the sink to remove seeds. Cut tomatoes into 1-inch dice, and set aside. Cut bread into ¹/₂-inch cubes, and place cubes in the slow cooker.

2. Heat oil in a medium skillet over medium-high heat. Add onion and garlic, and cook, stirring frequently, for 3 minutes, or until onion is translucent. Add tomatoes and cook an additional 5 minutes, or until tomatoes soften. Scrape mixture into the slow cooker.

3. Add milk and basil to the slow cooker, and stir well. Cook on Low for 4 to 6 hours or on High for 2 to 3 hours, stirring midway through the cooking time, or until mixture is thick and creamy.

4. If cooking on Low, raise the heat to High. Stir mozzarella and Parmesan cheeses into the slow cooker, and cook for an additional 10 to 15 minutes, or until cheeses melt. Season to taste with salt and pepper, and serve hot, garnishing each serving with additional basil leaves.

Note: The dish can be prepared up to 2 days in advance and refrigerated, tightly covered. Reheat it, covered, in a 350°F oven for 20 to 25 minutes, or until hot.

Variation:

* Substitute Gorgonzola for the Parmesan, and substitute rosemary for the basil.

> There is a tremendous difference in flavor between whole milk mozzarella and the more popular part-skimmed milk version. The dish will suffer if you use the latter cheese.

Vegetable Soup with Clams

This soup is like an Italian version of Manhattan clam chowder. While in Italy it's served with tiny whole clams, I think it's more "eater-friendly" with minced clams.

Makes 6 to 8 servings | Prep time: 15 minutes | Minimum cook time: 3 hours in a medium slow cooker

1 pint minced fresh clams

2 tablespoons olive oil

2 anchovy fillets, finely chopped

1 small onion, diced

2 garlic cloves, minced

1 celery rib, diced

1 carrot, finely chopped

½ green bell pepper, seeds and ribs removed, and chopped

2 large redskin potatoes, scrubbed and cut into ¾-inch dice

1 (14.5-ounce) can crushed tomatoes, undrained

1 (8-ounce) bottle clam juice

1 cup dry white wine

1 tablespoon capers, drained and rinsed

3 tablespoons chopped fresh parsley

1 tablespoon fresh thyme or ½ teaspoon dried

2 teaspoons fresh oregano or ½ teaspoon dried

2 bay leaves

Salt and freshly ground black pepper to taste

1. Drain clams, reserving juice. Refrigerate clams until ready to use.

2. Heat oil in a medium skillet over medium heat. Add anchovies, onion, garlic, celery, carrot, and green bell pepper. Cook, stirring frequently, for 3 minutes, or until onion is translucent. Scrape mixture into the slow cooker.

3. Add potatoes, tomatoes, clam juice, wine, capers, juice drained from clams, parsley, thyme, oregano, and bay leaves to the slow cooker, and stir well. Cook on Low for 5 to 7 hours or on High for 2½ to 3 hours, or until potatoes are almost tender.

4. If cooking on Low, raise the heat to High. Add clams, and continue to cook for an additional 20 to 40 minutes, or until clams are cooked through. Remove and discard bay leaves, season to taste with salt and pepper, and serve hot.

Note: The soup can be prepared up to 3 days in advance and refrigerated, tightly covered. Reheat it, covered, over low heat, stirring occasionally.

Variations:

✻ Substitute 1 pound of firm-fleshed white fish like cod or halibut, cut into ⅓-inch dice, for the clams.

✻ Substitute ¾ pound squid, cleaned and cut into ½-inch rings for the clams, and add an additional ½ cup clam juice to the soup.

✻ Start by cooking ¼ pound chopped pancetta until crisp. Substitute 2 tablespoons of the fat for the olive oil, and add the cooked pancetta to the soup when the clams are added.

> It's now possible to find fresh minced clams in just about every supermarket. If they're not in the refrigerated case, check the freezer. If you must resort to canned clams, use 3 (6-ounce) cans for each pint of fresh clams specified.

Chicken Soup with Fennel and Escarole

The licorice flavor of fresh fennel is reinforced by fennel seeds in this easy Italian healthful chicken soup.

Makes 6 to 8 servings | Prep time: 20 minutes | Minimum cook time: 3 hours in a medium slow cooker

1 pound boneless, skinless chicken meat

1 large fennel bulb

3 tablespoons olive oil

2 large onions, diced

3 garlic cloves, minced

5 cups Chicken Stock (page 19) or purchased stock

1 (14.5-ounce) can diced tomatoes, undrained

2 teaspoons fennel seeds, crushed

1 head escarole

Salt and freshly ground black pepper to taste

½ cup freshly grated Parmesan cheese

1. Rinse chicken and pat dry with paper towels. Trim chicken of all visible fat, and cut into ½-inch cubes. Rinse fennel and cut in half lengthwise. Discard core and ribs. Dice bulb into ¾-inch pieces. Place chicken and fennel in the slow cooker.

2. Heat olive oil in a medium skillet over medium-high heat. Add onions and garlic, and cook, stirring frequently, for 3 minutes, or until onions are translucent. Scrape mixture into the slow cooker.

3. Stir stock, tomatoes, and fennel seeds into the slow cooker, and stir well. Cook on Low for 5 to 7 hours or on High for 2½ to 3 hours, or until chicken is cooked through and no longer pink. While soup cooks, rinse escarole and discard core. Slice escarole into strips 1-inch wide.

4. If cooking on Low, raise the heat to High. Add escarole to the slow cooker, and cook for an additional 30 to 40 minutes, or until escarole is wilted. Season to taste with salt and pepper, and serve hot, passing cheese separately.

Note: The soup can be prepared up to 3 days in advance and refrigerated, tightly covered. Reheat it, covered, over low heat, stirring occasionally.

Variation:
✳ Substitute Swiss chard for the escarole.

> Fresh fennel, *finocchio* in Italian, and sometimes called anise in supermarkets, has a slightly licorice taste but the texture of celery—both raw and cooked. You can always substitute 2 celery ribs for each ½ fennel bulb specified in a recipe.

Bean, Corn, and Barley Soup

Barley is an ancient grain that is used in Italy's northern provinces. It creates a thick and robust soup flavored with many vegetables and herbs as well as delicate cannellini beans.

Makes 6 to 8 servings | Prep time: 20 minutes | Minimum cook time: 4 hours in a medium slow cooker

1 tablespoon olive oil

½ cup finely chopped pancetta

1 large onion, diced

3 garlic cloves, minced

1 celery rib, diced

¾ cup pearl barley, rinsed well

5 cups Chicken Stock (page 19) or purchased stock

¼ cup chopped fresh parsley

1 tablespoon chopped fresh rosemary or 1 teaspoon dried

1 bay leaf

1 (15-ounce) can cannellini beans, drained and rinsed

¾ cup fresh corn kernels, or frozen kernels, thawed

⅔ cup freshly grated Parmesan cheese

Salt and freshly ground black pepper to taste

1. Heat oil in a large skillet over medium-high heat. Add pancetta, and cook for 4 to 5 minutes, or until lightly brown. Add onion, garlic, and celery, and cook, stirring frequently, for 3 minutes, or until onion is translucent. Scrape mixture into the slow cooker.

2. Add barley, stock, parsley, rosemary, and bay leaf to the slow cooker, and stir well. Cook on Low for 6 to 8 hours or High for 3 to 4 hours, or until vegetables are tender. If cooking on Low, raise the heat to High. Stir beans, corn, and Parmesan into the slow cooker, and cook for 20 to 30 minutes, or until cheese melts.

3. Remove and discard bay leaf, season to taste with salt and pepper, and serve hot.

Note: The soup can be prepared up to 3 days in advance and refrigerated, tightly covered. Reheat it, covered, over low heat, stirring occasionally. More stock or water might have to be added if the soup is chilled; the barley keeps absorbing liquid after cooking.

Variations:
* Substitute kidney beans for the cannellini beans.

Barley is one of the foods prohibited on a gluten-free diet. If cooking for someone on this diet, the best substitute for barley is either quinoa or buckwheat. They will cook in the same amount of time, although the soup will not be as thick.

White Bean Soup with Prosciutto and Spinach

This is my all-time favorite bean soup, with flecks of salty prosciutto and bits of bright green spinach in a thick and flavorful base of beans.

Makes 6 to 8 servings | *Prep time: 15 minutes* | *Minimum cook time: 4 hours in a medium slow cooker*

2 cups dried navy beans or other small dried white beans

2 teaspoons salt

3 tablespoons olive oil

1 large onion, diced

2 garlic cloves, minced

1 large carrot, chopped

2 celery ribs, minced

1 (14.5-ounce) can diced tomatoes, drained

1 cup chopped prosciutto

6 cups Chicken Stock (page 19) or purchased stock

3 tablespoons chopped fresh parsley

2 tablespoons chopped fresh rosemary or 2 teaspoons dried

¼ pound fresh spinach, rinsed and stemmed

Salt and freshly ground black pepper to taste

Freshly grated Parmesan cheese to taste

1. Rinse beans in a colander and place them in a mixing bowl covered with 1 quart cold water mixed with salt. Allow beans to soak for at least six hours, or overnight. Or place beans into a saucepan with water and salt, and bring to a boil over high heat. Boil 1 minute. Turn off the heat, cover the pan, and soak beans for 1 hour. With either soaking method, drain beans, discard soaking water, and begin cooking as soon as possible.

2. Heat olive oil in a medium skillet over medium-high heat. Add onion, garlic, carrot, and celery, and cook, stirring frequently, for 3 minutes, or until onion is translucent. Scrape mixture into the slow cooker.

3. Add drained beans, tomatoes, prosciutto, stock, parsley, and rosemary to the slow cooker, and stir well. Cook on Low for 8 to 10 hours or on High for 4 to 5 hours, or until beans are tender.

4. Using a slotted spoon, transfer half of solids to a food processor fitted with a steel blade or a blender, and puree until smooth. Stir puree back into soup, add spinach, and stir well. Cook on High for 20 to 30 minutes, or until soup is simmering. Season to taste with salt and pepper, and serve hot, passing Parmesan cheese separately.

Note: The soup can be prepared up to 3 days in advance and refrigerated, tightly covered. Reheat it, covered, over low heat, stirring occasionally.

Variation:

❋ Substitute Swiss chard for the spinach; the cooking time will remain the same.

Prosciutto has been made for more than 2,000 years in the region of Italy near Parma and must come from Parma, San Daniele, or the Veneto to be authentic. If you've wondered why prosciutto seems to go so well with Parmesan cheese, it might be because the whey from making Parmigiano Reggiano is one of the foods fed to the pigs prosciutto comes from.

Sausage and Chestnut Soup

I first had this soup at Lidia Bastinach's fabulous Felidia restaurant in New York, and the creamy, earthy chestnuts laced with a bit of heady Marsala is a wonderful base for the bits of sausage.

Makes 4 to 6 servings | Prep time: 20 minutes | Minimum cook time: 2 $\frac{1}{2}$ hours in a medium slow cooker

3 tablespoons unsalted butter

1 small onion, chopped

1 celery rib, chopped

1 small carrot, chopped

1 garlic clove, minced

6 cups Chicken Stock (page 19) or purchased stock

2 tablespoons chopped fresh parsley

1 tablespoon chopped fresh rosemary or 1 teaspoon dried

1 bay leaf

1 (15-ounce) jar cooked chestnuts, chopped

⅓ cup sweet Marsala

½ cup heavy cream

1 tablespoon olive oil

½ pound bulk sweet Italian sausage

Salt and freshly ground black pepper to taste

1. Heat butter in a small skillet over medium-high heat. Add onion, celery, carrot, and garlic. Cook, stirring frequently, for 3 minutes, or until onion is translucent. Scrape mixture into the slow cooker.

2. Add stock, parsley, rosemary, bay leaf, chestnuts, and Marsala to the slow cooker, and stir well. Cook on Low for 4½ to 6 hours or on High for 2 to 3 hours, or until vegetables are tender. Then, if cooking on Low, raise the heat to High. Add cream, and cook soup for an additional 20 to 25 minutes, or until simmering.

3. While soup simmers, heat oil in a skillet over medium-high heat. Crumble sausage into the skillet and cook, breaking up lumps with a fork, for 3 to 5 minutes, or until browned. Set aside.

4. Allow soup to cool for 10 minutes. Remove and discard bay leaf. Either puree it with an immersion blender, or strain solids from soup and puree them in a food processor fitted with the steel blade or in a blender. Season to taste with salt and pepper, and serve hot, garnishing each serving with sausage.

Note: The soup can be prepared up to 3 days in advance and refrigerated, tightly covered. Reheat it, covered, over low heat, stirring occasionally.

Variation:
＊ Substitute golden sherry for the marsala.

Marsala is a fortified wine, similar to Madeira and sherry, made in Sicily from a variety of grapes grown around the town of Marsala. It was very popular with the English market in the early nineteenth century after Lord Nelson made it his choice as an onboard drink.

Potato Soup with Pancetta and Gorgonzola

The essentially mild flavor of potatoes makes them a natural to blend with cheeses, especially assertive cheeses like heady Gorgonzola. The bits of pancetta add a smoky note too.

Makes 6 to 8 servings | *Active time: 20 minutes* | *Minimum cook time: 4 hours in a medium slow cooker*

¼ pound pancetta, diced

1 medium onion, diced

1 carrot, diced

1 celery rib, diced

1 garlic clove, minced

1 pound Russet potatoes, peeled and cut into ¾-inch dice

4 cups Chicken Stock (page 19) or purchased stock

2 teaspoons fresh thyme or ½ teaspoon dried

1 cup crumbled Gorgonzola

½ cup grated fontina

1 cup half-and-half

Salt and freshly ground black pepper to taste

1. Cook pancetta in a skillet over medium-high heat, stirring frequently, for 4 to 5 minutes, or until browned. Remove pancetta from the pan with a slotted spoon, drain on paper towels, and set aside. Discard all but 3 tablespoons grease from the skillet.

2. Add onion, carrot, celery, and garlic to the skillet, and cook, stirring frequently, for 3 minutes, or until onion is translucent. Scrape mixture into the slow cooker.

3. Add potatoes, stock, and thyme to the slow cooker, and stir well. Cook on Low for 6 to 8 hours or on High for 3 to 4 hours, or until vegetables are tender.

4. If cooking on Low, raise the heat to High. Mash some of vegetables with a potato masher until desired consistency; the more that is mashed the thicker the soup will be. Add Gorgonzola, fontina, and half-and-half, and cook for 20 to 30 minutes, or until cheeses melt and soup simmers. Season to taste with salt and pepper, and serve hot, sprinkling each serving with pancetta.

Note: The soup can be prepared up to 3 days in advance and refrigerated, tightly covered. Reheat it, covered, over low heat, stirring occasionally.

Variations:

❋ Substitute Parmesan for the Gorgonzola.

❋ Add ¼ cup cloves from Roasted Garlic (page 47) to the slow cooker.

> The blue veins that appear in blue cheeses such as Gorgonzola and Stilton is actually a mold that is a member of the penicillin family. In some cases the fresh cheese is injected with the mold spores, while in other cases the mold is mixed right into the curds.

Cabbage and Sausage Soup

Sausage should really be considered a convenience food because there are so many flavoring ingredients added to it during the grinding process. All those flavors are then transferred to this hearty soup.

Makes 4 to 6 servings | Active time: 20 minutes | Minimum cook time: 3½ hours in a medium slow cooker

½ pound bulk luganega, cotechino, or other raw Italian sausage

1 medium onion, diced

2 garlic cloves, minced

2 carrots, diced

4 cups firmly packed thinly sliced green cabbage

5 cups Chicken Stock (page 19) or purchased stock

1 (14.5-ounce) can diced tomatoes, undrained

2 tablespoons tomato paste

1 pound redskin potatoes, scrubbed and cut into ¾-inch dice

2 tablespoons chopped fresh parsley

1 tablespoon chopped fresh oregano or 1 teaspoon dried

1 tablespoon chopped fresh thyme or ½ teaspoon dried

Salt and freshly ground black pepper to taste

1. Heat a skillet over medium-high heat. Add sausage and cook, breaking up lumps with a fork, for 3 to 5 minutes, or until sausage is browned. Remove sausage from the pan with a slotted spoon, and transfer it to the slow cooker. Discard all but 2 tablespoons fat from the skillet.

2. Add onion, garlic, and carrots to the skillet, and cook, stirring frequently, for 3 minutes, or until onion is translucent. Add cabbage, and cook for an additional 2 minutes, or until cabbage begins to wilt. Scrape mixture into the slow cooker.

3. Add stock, tomatoes, tomato paste, potatoes, parsley, oregano, and thyme to the slow cooker, and stir well. Cook on Low for 7 to 9 hours or on High for 3½ to 4½ hours, or until potatoes are tender. Season to taste with salt and pepper, and serve hot.

Note: The soup can be prepared up to 3 days in advance and refrigerated, tightly covered. Reheat it, covered, over low heat, stirring occasionally.

Variation:
∗ Substitute ground pork or ground beef for the sausage for a milder soup.

Like many recipes, this one calls for 2 tablespoons tomato paste. I buy tomato paste that comes in a tube, which will keep refrigerated for a few months. If you do open a can, freeze the remaining sauce in 1-tablespoon portions in an ice cube tray lined with plastic wrap. Then store the small cubes in a heavy plastic bag for up to six months.

Italian Wedding Soup

Wedding soup is actually Italian-American rather than tied to any Italian region. It is a mistranslation of *minestra maritata,* which has nothing to do with nuptials, but is a reference to the fact that green vegetables and meats go well together.

Makes 6 to 8 servings | Prep time: 25 minutes | Minimum cook time: 3 hours in a medium slow cooker

4 large eggs, lightly beaten, divided

⅓ cup Italian breadcrumbs

¼ cup milk

¼ cup grated whole milk mozzarella cheese

5 garlic cloves, minced, divided

¾ pound ground pork

½ pound ground veal

Salt and freshly ground black pepper to taste

6 cups Chicken Stock (page 19) or purchased stock

1 fennel bulb, rinsed, trimmed, and thinly sliced

½ pound escarole, cored and coarsely chopped

½ cup orzo

½ cup freshly grated Parmesan, divided

Vegetable oil spray

1. Preheat the oven to 500°F. Line a broiler pan with heavy-duty aluminum foil, and grease the foil with vegetable oil spray or vegetable oil.

2. Combine 2 eggs, breadcrumbs, milk, cheese, and 2 garlic cloves into a mixing bowl, and whisk well. Add pork and veal, mix well, and season to taste with salt and pepper. Form mixture into 1-inch balls, and place them on the greased foil. Brown meatballs in the oven for 10 minutes, or until lightly browned. Transfer meatballs to the slow cooker with a slotted spoon.

3. Add stock, fennel, and remaining garlic to the slow cooker. Cook on Low for 6 to 8 hours or on High for 3 to 4 hours, or until meatballs are cooked through and fennel is soft.

4. If cooking on Low, raise the heat to High. Add escarole and orzo to the slow cooker. Cook on High for 20 to 30 minutes, or until orzo is cooked al dente. Season to taste with salt and pepper, and serve hot, passing cheese separately.

Note: The soup can be prepared up to 3 days in advance and refrigerated, tightly covered. Reheat it, covered, over low heat, stirring occasionally.

Variations:
* Substitute ground turkey for the pork and veal.
* Substitute curly endive for the escarole.

There is evidence to support the idea that chicken stock really does contain medicinal qualities; perhaps your grandma was right all along. In 1993, University of Nebraska Medical Center researcher Dr. Stephen Rennard published a study stating that chicken soup contains a number of substances including an anti-inflammatory mechanism that eases the symptoms of upper respiratory tract infections. Other studies also showed that the chicken soup was equally medicinal if made without vegetables; it was the chicken itself.

Vegetable Beef Soup with Pasta

A larger portion of this hearty soup could easily be a casual supper, served with some aromatic garlic bread and a tossed salad. It has a cornucopia of wonderful vegetables, as well as pasta and beans.

Makes 6 to 8 servings | Prep time: 25 minutes | Minimum cook time: 4 hours in a medium slow cooker

1¼ pounds stewing beef

2 tablespoons olive oil

1 large onion, diced

3 garlic cloves, minced

1½ cups shredded green cabbage

1 (14.5-ounce) can diced tomatoes, undrained

5 cups Beef Stock (page 21) or purchased stock

1 carrot, thinly sliced

1 celery rib, sliced

3 tablespoons fresh chopped parsley

2 tablespoons chopped fresh marjoram or 2 teaspoons dried

1 bay leaf

2 small zucchini, cut into ½-inch dice

¼ pound fresh green beans, trimmed and cut into ½-inch slices

1 (15-ounce) can white cannellini beans, drained and rinsed

¾ cup small elbow macaroni or small pasta shells, cooked according to package directions until al dente

Salt and freshly ground black pepper to taste

Freshly grated Parmesan cheese

1. Preheat the oven broiler, and line a broiler pan with heavy-duty aluminum foil. Rinse beef and pat dry with paper towels. Cut beef into ³⁄₄-inch cubes, if necessary. Broil cubes for 3 minutes per side, or until browned. Transfer beef to the slow cooker, and pour in any juices that have collected in the pan.

2. Heat olive oil in a medium skillet over medium-high heat. Add onion and garlic, and cook, stirring frequently, for 3 minutes, or until onion is translucent. Scrape mixture into the slow cooker.

3. Add cabbage, tomatoes, stock, carrot, celery, parsley, marjoram, and bay leaf to the slow cooker. Cook on Low for 6 to 8 hours or on High for 3 to 4 hours, or until vegetables are crisp-tender.

4. If cooking on Low, raise the heat to High. Stir in zucchini, green beans, and cannellini beans. Cook for 45 minutes to 1 hour, or until vegetables are soft. Stir in pasta to heat. Season to taste with salt and pepper, and serve hot, passing Parmesan cheese separately.

Note: The soup can be prepared up to 3 days in advance and refrigerated, tightly covered. Reheat it, covered, over low heat, stirring occasionally.

Variation:

❋ Substitute chicken for the beef; it is not necessary to brown it. And substitute chicken stock for the beef stock.

In Italy this soup would generally be made with wide and flat Roman beans, but those are difficult to find in our markets. Should you find them, they need about 10 minutes longer to cook than our common green beans.

Spicy Shrimp Scampi

This is a flavorful primi that is incredibly easy to make and always a hit. It's redolent with garlic, spicy from crushed red pepper, and brightly colored from a combination of paprika and parsley. Serve it in a scallop shell, if you have them.

Makes 6 to 8 servings | Prep time: 15 minutes | Minimum cook time: 1½ hours in a medium slow cooker

½ cup olive oil

6 garlic cloves, minced

1 tablespoon paprika

2 pounds extra-large (16 to 20 per pound) shrimp, peeled and deveined

½ cup dry white wine

3 tablespoons chopped fresh parsley

Salt and crushed red pepper flakes to taste

Lemon wedges for serving

1. Combine olive oil, garlic, paprika, shrimp, wine, and parsley in the slow cooker. Cook on Low for 3 to 4 hours or on High for 1½ to 2 hours, or until shrimp are pink and cooked through. Season to taste with salt and red pepper flakes.

2. Serve warm or at room temperature, and pass lemon wedges separately.

Note: The dish can be prepared up to 1 day in advance and refrigerated, tightly covered with plastic wrap. Allow it to sit at room temperature for 30 minutes before serving.

Variation:

＊ Substitute 1-inch cubes of cod or any firm-fleshed white fish for the shrimp.

When you buy shrimp that are still in their shells, they need to be peeled, and that's an obvious task. Step two is to devein them. In one hand, hold the shrimp with its back facing up. With the other hand, cut gently down the back with a small paring knife. If there is a thin black line, scrape it out. That's the "vein"—it's actually the intestinal tract—which can be bitter and gritty.

Steamed Mussels with Garlic Broth

Steamed mollusks are a favorite easy *primi* in most of southern Italy. Serve them with crusty bread.

Makes 4 to 6 servings | Prep time: 15 minutes | Minimum cook time: 1¹/₂ hours in a medium slow cooker

2 pounds live mussels

3 tablespoons olive oil

1 shallot, minced

3 garlic cloves, minced

¼ cup dry white wine

¼ cup chopped fresh parsley

Salt and freshly ground black pepper to taste

1. Just before cooking, clean mussels by scrubbing them well with a brush under cold water; discard any that do not shut tightly. Scrape off any barnacles with a knife. If beard is still attached, remove it by pulling it from tip to hinge, or by pulling and cutting it off with knife. Set aside.

2. Heat olive oil in a small skillet over medium heat. Add shallot and garlic and cook, stirring frequently, for 2 minutes, or until shallot is translucent. Scrape mixture into the slow cooker. Add ¹/₄ cup water, wine, and mussels. Cook on High for 1¹/₂ to 2 hours, or until mussels open. Shake the slow cooker a few times, without opening it, to redistribute mussels.

3. Remove mussels from the slow cooker with a slotted spoon, discarding any that did not open. Stir in parsley, and season to taste with salt and pepper. To serve, place mussels in shallow bowls and ladle broth on top. Serve with soup spoons as well as seafood forks.

Note: This dish should not be prepared in advance or reheated; however, the clams can be scrubbed up to 6 hours in advance.

Variations:

✳ Substitute 3 dozen littleneck or small cherrystone clams for the mussels.

✳ Add 1 teaspoon crushed red pepper flakes to the slow cooker with the mussels for a spicier dish.

Leftover broth from a recipe for steamed mollusks is a treasure trove of flavor for saucing future fish dishes. Freeze it, and be sure to note what dish it's from so you know what flavors you're adding.

Vegetable Frittata with Pasta

It's important that you cook the vegetables until they're dry. If they're not cooked to that point, the frittata will be watery and not come out of the pan easily.

Makes 6 to 8 servings | Prep time: 25 minutes | Minimum cook time: 2 hours in a medium slow cooker

1 (6-ounce) package refrigerated angel hair pasta

3 tablespoons olive oil

2 small zucchini, sliced

4 scallions, white parts and 3 inches of green tops, thinly sliced

3 garlic cloves, minced

2 ripe plum tomatoes, rinsed, cored, seeded, and finely chopped

3 tablespoons chopped fresh basil or 2 teaspoons dried

1 tablespoon chopped fresh oregano or 1 teaspoon dried

¼ cup sliced green olives

Salt and freshly ground black pepper to taste

6 large eggs

½ cup freshly grated Parmesan cheese

Vegetable oil spray

1. Cook pasta according to package directions until al dente. Drain and set aside to cool.

2. Heat oil in a large skillet over medium-high heat. Add zucchini, scallions, and garlic. Cook, stirring frequently, for 5 minutes, or until zucchini is tender. Add tomatoes, basil, oregano, and olives. Cook mixture, stirring frequently, for 5 minutes, or until liquid from tomatoes evaporates. Season to taste with salt and pepper, and cool for 10 minutes.

3. Grease the inside of the slow cooker liberally with vegetable oil spray or melted butter. Fold a sheet of heavy-duty aluminum foil in half, and place it in the bottom of the slow cooker with the sides of the foil extending up the sides of the slow cooker. Whisk eggs with cheese, and stir in cooked pasta and vegetables. Pour mixture into the slow cooker.

4. Cook on High for 2 to 2½ hours, or until eggs are set. Run a spatula around the sides of the slow cooker. Remove frittata from the slow cooker by pulling it up by the sides of the foil. Slide it gently onto a serving platter, and cut it into wedges. Serve hot, at room temperature, or chilled.

Note: The vegetable mixture can be cooked up to 1 day in advance and refrigerated, tightly covered. Reheat the vegetables to room temperature in a microwave-safe dish, or over low heat, before completing the dish.

Variations:

✳ Add ¾ cup chopped prosciutto or ham.

✳ Substitute ⅔ cup fresh peas or frozen peas, thawed, for 1 of the zucchini.

A frittata is basically a solid Italian omelet. While we bake frittatas, Italians fry them. The Italian word *frittata* is derived from the Latin *frigere*, which means "to fry." In Spain, the same dish is called a "tortilla," which bears no relationship to the thin corn or wheat pancakes eaten in Mexico and Central America.

Prosciutto and Spinach Frittata

Salty and silky prosciutto and toothsome spinach are a great combination to flavor this frittata. If you choose, a simple sauce such as Herbed Tomato Sauce (page 97) can be served on top.

Makes 6 to 8 servings | Active time: 15 minutes | Minimum cook time: 1¹/₂ hours in a medium slow cooker

2 tablespoons olive oil

1 medium onion, chopped

2 garlic cloves, minced

½ red bell pepper, seeds and ribs removed, and thinly sliced

1½ cups chopped prosciutto

8 large eggs

3 tablespoons whole milk

¾ cup frozen chopped spinach, thawed and drained well

¼ cup chopped pimiento-stuffed green olives

¼ cup freshly grated Parmesan cheese

2 tablespoons chopped fresh parsley

1 tablespoon fresh thyme or ½ teaspoon dried thyme

Salt and freshly ground black pepper to taste

Vegetable oil spray

1. Heat olive oil in a small skillet over medium-high heat. Add onion, garlic, red bell pepper, and prosciutto, and cook, stirring frequently, for 3 minutes, or until onion is translucent. Allow mixture to cool for 5 minutes.

2. Whisk eggs with milk in a mixing bowl. Stir in spinach, olives, Parmesan, parsley, thyme, and vegetable mixture. Season to taste with salt and pepper.

3. Grease the inside of the slow cooker insert liberally with vegetable oil spray or melted butter. Fold a sheet of heavy-duty aluminum foil in half, and place it in the bottom of the slow cooker with the sides of the foil extending up the sides of the slow cooker. Pour egg mixture into the slow cooker.

4. Cook on High for 2 to 2¹/₂ hours, or until eggs are set. Run a spatula around the sides of the slow cooker. Remove frittata from the slow cooker by pulling it up by the sides of the foil. Slide it gently onto a serving platter, and cut it into wedges. Serve immediately, or at room temperature.

Note: The vegetable mixture can be cooked up to 1 day in advance and refrigerated, tightly covered. Reheat the vegetables to room temperature in a microwave-safe dish, or over low heat, before completing the dish.

Variations:
* Substitute chopped baked ham or salami for the prosciutto.
* Substitute chopped broccoli, cooked according to package direction, for the spinach.

> When vegetables are prepared for freezing they are blanched in water. Frozen vegetables never need as much time to cook as their raw counterparts because they are partially pre-cooked. In the case of spinach, the blanching is all the cooking that is necessary, while other vegetables need additional time.

Mushroom and Sausage Frittata

Any combination of a vegetable and a meat are excellent for a frittata, and mushrooms and sausage are a classic that work well here. The rosemary adds an aromatic accent.

Makes 6 to 8 servings | Prep time: 20 minutes | Minimum cook time: 2 hours in a medium slow cooker

½ pound bulk sweet or hot Italian sausage

1 medium onion, diced

1 garlic clove, minced

¼ pound mushrooms, wiped with a damp paper towel, trimmed, and thinly sliced

8 large eggs

¼ cup half-and-half

½ cup grated whole milk mozzarella cheese

2 tablespoons chopped fresh parsley

1 tablespoon chopped fresh rosemary or 1 teaspoon dried

Salt and freshly ground black pepper to taste

Vegetable oil spray

1. Crumble sausage into a skillet over medium-high heat. Cook for 5 to 7 minutes, breaking up lumps with a fork, or until sausage is browned. Remove sausage from the pan with a slotted spoon, drain on paper towels, and set aside.

2. Discard all but 3 tablespoons sausage fat from the skillet. Add onion, garlic, and mushrooms, and cook for 5 to 7 minutes, or until mushrooms are brown and the liquid has evaporated from the skillet. Allow mixture to cool for 10 minutes.

3. Whisk eggs with half-and-half in a mixing bowl. Stir in cheese, parsley, and rosemary, and season with salt and pepper. Add sausage and cooled vegetable mixture, and stir well.

4. Grease the inside of the slow cooker insert liberally with vegetable oil spray or melted butter. Fold a sheet of heavy-duty aluminum foil in half, and place it in the bottom of the slow cooker with the sides of the foil extending up the sides of the slow cooker. Pour egg mixture into the slow cooker.

5. Cook on High for 2 to 2½ hours, or until eggs are set. Run a spatula around the sides of the slow cooker. Remove frittata from the slow cooker by pulling it up by the sides of the foil. Slide it gently onto a serving platter, and cut it into wedges. Serve immediately, at room temperature, or chilled.

Note: The sausage and the vegetable mixture can be cooked up to 1 day in advance and refrigerated, tightly covered. Reheat them to room temperature in a microwave-safe dish, or over low heat, before completing the dish.

Variations:

❋ Substitute ¼ pound thinly sliced zucchini or yellow squash for the mushrooms.

❋ Substitute chopped ham for the sausage, and sauté the vegetables in 2 tablespoons olive oil.

> Mushrooms have to be pre-cooked to remove all their inherent water for a dish such as this frittata. It would be watery if they were added raw. The same is not true, however, for stews or soups. For those, the mushrooms can cook with the rest of the dish.

Chapter 4

Sauces for Pasta

Plus Risotto and Polenta as Primi

*I*talian pasta preparations fall into two distinct camps. Some, like tossing the cooked pasta with garlic and olive oil, take merely seconds. Creating the depth of flavor achieved in a sauce that's simmered for hours, especially tomato-based sauces, are where the slow cooker enters into the equation. These same slowly cooked sauces are also excellent to top creamy polenta, which cannot be topped with a quick sauté for the obvious reason. Those are the recipes you'll find in this chapter. At the end of the chapter are recipes for polenta and risotto, always appropriate to serve instead of pasta.

With the increasing popularity of Italian food, we are coming full cycle and realizing that supple fresh pastas are not the best match for many hearty sauces, and there is always a place in the pantry for a box of dried. Good-quality dried pasta is made with a high percentage of high-gluten semolina, the inner part of the grain of hard durum wheat. The gluten gives the pasta resilience and allows it to cook while remaining somewhat firm, the elusive *al dente*.

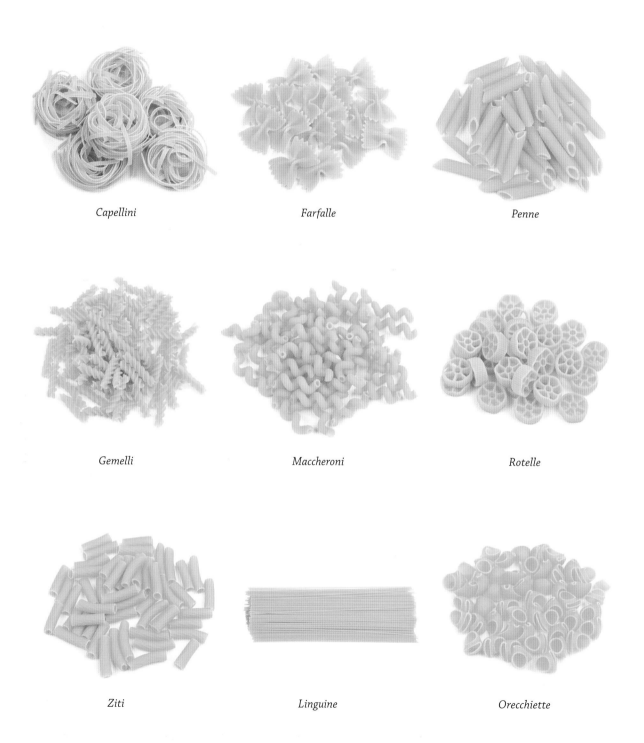

Capellini

Farfalle

Penne

Gemelli

Maccheroni

Rotelle

Ziti

Linguine

Orecchiette

Many pasta recipes are written for specific pasta shapes. But there is wide latitude for substitution. What's important is to find pasta of about the same dimensions that cooks in the same amount of time.

Those are your guides to matching a shape with a sauce. Here are the types of dried pasta found most often:

Dried Pasta

NAME (MEANING)	DESCRIPTION	COOKING TIME
Anelli (Rings)	Medium, ridged tubes cut into thin rings	6–8 min.
Cannelloni (Large Pipes)	Large cylinders	8–10 min. with further baking
Capellini (Hair)	Thinnest strands	2–4 min.
Cavatappi (Corkscrews)	Short ridged pasta twisted into a spiral	8–10 min.
Conchiglie (Shells)	Shells about 1-inch long	8–10 min.
Ditalini (Little Thimbles)	Very short round pieces	6–9 min.
Farfalle (Butterflies)	Flat rectangles pinched in the center to form a bow	10–12 min.
Fettuccine (Little Ribbons)	Long, flat ribbon shapes, about $1/4$-inch wide	6–9 min.
Fusilli (Twisted Spaghetti)	Long, spring-shaped strands	10–12 min.
Gemilli (Twins)	Medium strands woven together and cut into 2-inch lengths	8–10 min.
Linguine (Little Tongues)	Thin, slightly flattened solid strands about $1/8$-inch wide	6–9 min.

Maccheroni (Macaroni)	Thin, tubular pasta in various widths	8–10 min.
Manicotti (Small Muffs)	Thick, ridged tubes	10–12 min.
Mostaccioli (Small Mustaches)	Medium-sized tubes with angle-cut ends	8–10 min.
Orecchiette (Ears)	Smooth, curved rounds about $\frac{1}{2}$-inch in diameter	6–9 min.
Orzo (Barley)	Tiny, rice-shaped	6–9 min.
Penne (Quills)	Small tubes with angle-cut ends	8–10 min.
Radiatore (Radiators)	Short, thick, and ruffled	8–10 min.
Rigatoni (Large Grooved)	Thick, ridged tubes about $1\frac{1}{2}$-inches long	10–12 min.
Riso (Rice)	Tiny grains	4–6 min.
Rotelle (Wheels)	Spiral-shaped with spokes	8–10 min.
Rotini (Spirals)	Two thick strands twisted	8–10 min.
Spaghetti (Length of Cord)	Thin long strands	8–10 min.
Vermicelli (Little Worms)	Thinner than spaghetti	6–8 min.
Ziti (Bridegroom)	Medium-sized tubes about about 2-inches long	10–12 min.

Vegetarian Bolognese Sauce

I really wanted to create a vegetarian sauce that had the same gusto, and provided the same satisfying comfort, as my Bolognese sauce made with meat. I hope you'll agree that this sauce delivers. It has a wide range of vegetables as well as seasonings.

Makes 6 to 8 servings | Prep time: 15 minutes | Minimum cook time: 3 hours in a medium slow cooker

¼ cup olive oil

1 large onion, diced

5 garlic cloves, minced

¾ pound mushrooms, wiped with a damp paper towel, trimmed, and sliced

1 large carrot, chopped

2 celery ribs, chopped

1 (10-ounce) package frozen chopped spinach, thawed and drained

¼ cup chopped fresh parsley

2 tablespoons chopped fresh oregano or 2 teaspoons dried

1 tablespoon fresh thyme or ½ teaspoon dried

2 bay leaves

2 (28-ounce) cans crushed tomatoes

1 cup dry red wine

3 tablespoons tomato paste

Salt and freshly ground black pepper to taste

1. Heat oil in a large skillet over medium-high heat. Add onion, garlic, and mushrooms, and cook, stirring frequently, for 5 to 7 minutes, or until mushrooms soften. Scrape mixture into the slow cooker.

2. Add carrot, celery, spinach, parsley, oregano, thyme, bay leaves, tomatoes, wine, and tomato paste to the slow cooker. Stir well.

3. Cook on Low for 6 to 8 hours or on High for 3 to 4 hours, or until vegetables are soft. Remove and discard bay leaves, and season to taste with salt and pepper.

Note: The sauce can be prepared up to 2 days in advance and refrigerated, tightly covered. Reheat it, covered, over low heat, stirring occasionally.

Variations:

❋ Substitute 1 large green or red bell pepper, seeds and ribs removed, and diced, for the spinach. Cook the pepper with the other vegetables in Step 1.

❋ Substitute ¾ pound Italian eggplant, cut into ¾-inch cubes, for the spinach. Cook the eggplant with the other vegetables in Step 1.

> Cooked pasta is best reheated in a microwave oven, which will not toughen it. Microwave the pasta covered at full power for 1 minute. Check the temperature, and then continue to reheat at 30-second intervals.

Herbed Tomato Sauce

Here is your basic tomato sauce, similar to marinara sauce, which is perfect tossed with pasta or as topping for simple broiled or grilled foods.

Makes 6 to 8 servings | Prep time: 20 minutes | Minimum cook time: 4 hours in a medium slow cooker

¼ cup olive oil

1 large onion, chopped

½ red bell pepper, seeds and ribs removed, and chopped

2 garlic cloves, minced

1 (28-ounce) can crushed tomatoes

1 (6-ounce) can tomato paste

½ cup dry white wine

2 tablespoons chopped fresh oregano or 2 teaspoon dried

2 tablespoons chopped fresh basil or 2 teaspoon dried

1 tablespoon chopped fresh rosemary or 1 teaspoon dried

1 bay leaf

Salt and freshly ground black pepper to taste

1. Heat oil in a medium skillet over medium-high heat. Add onion, bell pepper, and garlic. Cook, stirring frequently, for 3 minutes, or until onion is translucent. Scrape the mixture into the slow cooker.

2. Add tomatoes, tomato paste, wine, $1/2$ cup water, oregano, basil, rosemary, and bay leaf to the slow cooker, and stir well. Cook on Low for 6 to 8 hours or on High for 3 to 4 hours, or until vegetables are tender.

3. If cooking on Low, raise the heat to High. Cook sauce, uncovered, for 1 hour, stirring occasionally, or until slightly thickened. Remove and discard bay leaf, and season to taste with salt and pepper.

Note: The sauce can be prepared up to 4 days in advance and refrigerated, tightly covered. It can also be frozen for up to 3 months.

Variations:

* Substitute red wine for the white wine.
* Add 1 pound raw medium shrimp, peeled and deveined, and $1/2$ pound bay scallops to the slow cooker for the last hour of cooking.

For many recipes you only need a few tablespoons or a partial cup of tomato sauce, so why not freeze a batch in different sized containers? That way you'll know that the half pint container is 1 cup and a pint is 2 cups.

Chicken and Olive Sauce

Olives are used extensively in Southern Italian pasta sauces, and they add robust flavor to this sauce made with healthful chicken and many fresh herbs.

Makes 6 to 8 servings | Prep time: 15 minutes | Minimum cook time: 3 hours in a medium slow cooker

2 tablespoons olive oil

1½ pounds boneless, skinless chicken thighs, cut into ¾-inch cubes

1 large onion, diced

3 garlic cloves, minced

½ teaspoon crushed red pepper flakes, or to taste

¾ cup Chicken Stock (page 19) or purchased stock

1 (14.5-ounce) can diced tomatoes, undrained

1 (15-ounce) can tomato sauce

½ cup dry white wine

1 tablespoon fresh thyme or ½ teaspoon dried

1 tablespoon chopped fresh rosemary or 1 teaspoon dried

¾ cup chopped pitted kalamata olives

3 tablespoons chopped fresh parsley

2 teaspoons grated lemon zest

Salt and freshly ground black pepper to taste

1. Heat oil in a skillet over medium-high heat. Add chicken and cook for 2 minutes, or until chicken is opaque. Transfer chicken to the slow cooker with a slotted spoon. Add onion, garlic, and red pepper flakes to the skillet. Cook, stirring frequently, for 3 minutes, or until onion is translucent. Scrape mixture into the slow cooker.

2. Add stock, tomatoes, tomato sauce, wine, thyme, and rosemary to the slow cooker. Stir well.

3. Cook on Low for 6 to 8 hours or on High for 3 to 4 hours, or until chicken is cooked through and tender. If cooking on Low, raise the heat to High. Add the olives, parsley, and lemon zest, and cook for 10 to 20 minutes, or until bubbling. Season to taste with salt and pepper.

Note: The sauce can be prepared up to 4 days in advance and refrigerated, tightly covered. It can also be frozen for up to 3 months.

Variation:
∗ Substitute boneless pork loin for the chicken. The cooking time will remain the same.

> The best way to shop for olives is at the olive bar or antipasto bar in your supermarket. You'll find the greatest variety, and you can purchase just the amount you need.

Bolognese Sauce

Unlike garlicky Italian-American "red sauce," a true Bolognese sauce is seasoned with restraint. What makes the sauce is simmering it with the combination of milk and white wine, which makes it smooth and tenderizes the meats.

Makes 6 to 8 servings | Prep time: 15 minutes | Minimum cook time: 4 hours in a medium slow cooker

3 tablespoons olive oil, divided

1 pound lean ground beef

½ pound lean ground pork

1 medium onion, diced

2 garlic cloves, minced (optional)

1 large carrot, chopped

2 celery ribs, chopped

1 (28-ounce) can crushed tomatoes

¾ cup whole milk

½ cup dry white wine

3 tablespoons chopped fresh parsley

1 tablespoon chopped fresh rosemary or 1 teaspoon dried

1 tablespoon fresh thyme or ½ teaspoon dried

2 bay leaves

Salt and freshly ground black pepper to taste

1. Heat 1 tablespoon oil in a large skillet over medium-high heat. Crumble beef and pork into the skillet, and cook for 3 minutes, breaking up lumps with a fork. Transfer meats to the slow cooker with a slotted spoon, discard fat, and wipe out the skillet with paper towels.

2. Heat remaining oil in the skillet over medium-high heat. Add onion, garlic (if using), carrot, and celery. Cook, stirring frequently, for 3 minutes, or until onion is translucent. Scrape mixture into the slow cooker.

3. Add tomatoes, milk, wine, parsley, rosemary, thyme, and bay leaves to the slow cooker. Stir well.

4. Cook on Low for 6 to 8 hours or on High for 3 to 4 hours, or until meats are tender. If cooking on Low, raise the heat to High. Uncover the slow cooker, and cook for 1 hour. Remove and discard bay leaves, and season to taste with salt and pepper.

Note: The sauce can be prepared up to 4 days in advance and refrigerated, tightly covered. It can also be frozen for up to 3 months.

Variations:
* Substitute pork sausage for the pork.
* Add $^1/_2$ cup chopped dry porcini mushrooms to the slow cooker.
* Cook 2 ounces chopped pancetta with the beef and pork.

The ancestors of the Bolognese sauce we know today date back to the fifth century in Bologna. The addition of tomatoes to the sauce came in the sixteenth century after the discovery of the New World. In Bologna the sauce is traditionally served with fresh tagliatelle rather than spaghetti, as well as for the layering of lasagna.

Beef and Sausage Ragù

This sauce is the epitome to me of what I want to eat on a frosty winter night. The combination of rich beef and flavorful sausage is the ultimate comfort food. It's also excellent topping polenta.

Makes 6 to 8 servings | Prep time: 20 minutes | Minimum cook time: 4 hours in a medium slow cooker

1 pound boneless short ribs of beef or stewing beef, cut into ¾-inch cubes

1 tablespoon olive oil

1 pound bulk sweet or hot Italian sausage

1 large onion, diced

3 garlic cloves, minced

½ pound white mushrooms, wiped with a damp paper towel, stemmed, and sliced

1 (28-ounce) can crushed tomatoes

1 cup dry red wine

2 tablespoons chopped fresh oregano or 2 teaspoons dried

2 bay leaves

2 teaspoons fennel seeds, crushed

¼ cup chopped fresh parsley

Salt and freshly ground black pepper to taste

1. Preheat the oven broiler, and line a broiler pan with heavy-duty aluminum foil. Broil beef for 3 minutes per side or until browned. Transfer beef to the slow cooker, and pour in any juices that have collected in the pan.

2. Heat olive oil in a medium skillet over medium-high heat. Crumble sausage into the skillet, and cook for 3 to 4 minutes, or until browned. Transfer sausage to the slow cooker with a slotted spoon.

3. Add onion, garlic, and mushrooms to the skillet. Cook, stirring frequently, for 4 to 5 minutes, or until onion is translucent and mushrooms soften. Scrape mixture into the slow cooker.

4. Add tomatoes, wine, oregano, bay leaves, and fennel seeds to the slow cooker. Stir well.

5. Cook on Low for 8 to 10 hours or on High for 4 to 5 hours, or until meat is very tender. Remove and discard bay leaves, stir in parsley, and season to taste with salt and pepper.

Note: The sauce can be prepared up to 4 days in advance and refrigerated, tightly covered. It can also be frozen for up to 3 months.

Variations:
* Substitute boneless lamb shoulder for the beef.
* Substitute boneless country ribs for the beef, and substitute white wine for the red wine.

Truffled Wild Mushroom Meat Sauce

Using both dried and fresh fungi in this hearty sauce from the Piedmont reinforces the earthy flavor of wild mushrooms. They are really the stars of this dish.

Makes 6 to 8 servings | Prep time: 15 minutes | Minimum cook time: 3 hours in a medium slow cooker

¾ cup dried porcini mushrooms

2½ cups Beef Stock (page 21) or purchased stock

3 tablespoons olive oil, divided

1 pound lean ground beef

2 tablespoons unsalted butter

3 shallots, diced

3 garlic cloves, minced

1 pound mixed fresh mushrooms, some combination of white, cremini, portobello, shiitake, and oyster), stemmed if necessary and sliced if large

2 teaspoons fresh thyme or ½ teaspoon dried

2 teaspoons cornstarch

½ cup heavy whipping cream

Salt and freshly ground black pepper to taste

2 tablespoons white truffle oil

1. Combine dried porcini mushrooms and stock in a small saucepan. Bring to a boil over high heat, remove the pan from the heat, and allow mushrooms to soak for 10 minutes. Remove mushrooms from stock with a slotted spoon, and chop. Strain stock through a sieve lined with a paper coffee filter or paper towel. Add mushrooms and stock to the slow cooker.

2. While mushrooms soak, heat 1 tablespoon oil in a large skillet over medium-high heat. Crumble beef into the skillet, and cook for 3 minutes, breaking up lumps with a fork. Transfer beef to the slow cooker with a slotted spoon, discard fat, and wipe out the skillet with paper towels.

3. Heat remaining oil and butter in the skillet over medium-high heat. Add shallots, garlic, mushrooms, and thyme. Cook, stirring frequently, for 5 to 7 minutes, or until mushrooms are soft. Scrape mixture into the slow cooker.

4. Cook on Low for 6 to 8 hours or on High for 3 to 4 hours, or until beef and mushrooms are tender. If cooking on Low, raise the heat to High. Combine cornstarch and cream, and stir well. Add mixture to the slow cooker and cook for 15 to 25 minutes, or until bubbling and slightly thickened. Season to taste with salt and pepper, and drizzle truffle oil over each serving.

Note: The sauce can be prepared up to 4 days in advance and refrigerated, tightly covered. It can also be frozen for up to 3 months.

Variation:

❋ Substitute ground turkey for the beef, and substitute chicken stock for the beef stock.

Fontina Polenta

Polenta is a relative newcomer to the world of Italian cuisine because all corn was imported from the New World. But it's now a gluten-free staple and can be adapted to many cuisines and times of day. Serve polenta instead of an English muffin as the base for eggs Benedict, or make it American and serve it at breakfast in place of grits.

Makes 4 to 6 servings | Prep time: 10 minutes | Minimum cook time: 3 hours in a medium slow cooker

5 cups Chicken Stock (page 19) or purchased stock

1 cup half-and-half

1 cup polenta or yellow cornmeal

3 tablespoons unsalted butter, cut into small pieces

1 cup grated Fontina cheese

Salt and freshly ground black pepper to taste

Vegetable oil spray

1. Grease the inside of the slow cooker liberally with vegetable oil spray.

2. Combine stock, half-and-half, and polenta in the slow cooker. Whisk well, and cook on High for 1½ hours, or until mixture begins to boil.

3. Whisk well again, and cook on High for an additional 1½ hours or on Low for 3 hours or until polenta is very thick.

4. Stir in butter and cheese, and season to taste with salt and pepper. Serve immediately as a side dish or topped with sauce. The polenta can remain on Warm for up to 4 hours.

Note: The dish can be prepared up to 2 days in advance and refrigerated, tightly covered. Reheat it, covered, in a 350°F oven for 20 to 25 minutes, or until hot.

Variations:

* Add 2 tablespoons chopped fresh herbs, such as sage, rosemary, or thyme at the onset of the cooking time.
* Add ½ cup dried porcini mushrooms, broken into small pieces and rinsed, to the slow cooker, and stir in 1 tablespoon truffle oil at the end of the cooking time.
* Add 1 (14.5-ounce) can diced tomatoes, undrained; 1 tablespoon tomato paste; and 2 tablespoons chopped fresh basil or oregano to the slow cooker, and reduce the amount of stock to 3 cups.
* Add 1 cup fresh corn kernels or frozen corn, thawed, to the slow cooker when whisking the polenta halfway through the cooking time.

An alternative way to serve polenta is to pack the hot polenta into a well-oiled loaf pan and chill it well. Once chilled you can cut it into ³/₄-inch slices and either grill them or saute them in butter or olive oil. You can also spread the polenta in a shallow baking dish to a thickness of ³/₄ inch, and then chill the mixture, cut it into long narrow rectangles, and pan-fry them.

Risotto

I could write a whole book on just variations of risotto, and once you've made it in the slow cooker you'll never stand at a stove stirring again. The quantity made by this recipe creates a side dish, either served as the pasta course or alongside a simple piece of fish, poultry, or meat. However, if you want to serve it as the entrée itself, double the recipe.

Makes 4 to 6 servings | Prep time: 15 minutes | Minimum cook time: 2 hours in a medium slow cooker

3 tablespoons unsalted butter

1 medium onion, chopped

1 cup Arborio rice

½ cup dry white wine

2½ cups Chicken Stock (page 19) or purchased stock

½ cup freshly grated Parmesan cheese

Salt and freshly ground black pepper to taste

1. Heat butter in a medium saucepan over medium-high heat. Add onion and cook, stirring frequently, for 3 minutes, or until onion is translucent. Add rice and stir to coat grains. Raise the heat to high and add wine. Stir for 2 minutes, or until wine is almost evaporated. Scrape mixture into the slow cooker.

2. Add stock to the slow cooker, and stir well. Cook on High for 2 hours, or until rice is soft and liquid is absorbed. Stir in cheese, season to taste with salt and pepper, and serve hot.

Note: The dish can be prepared up to 2 days in advance and refrigerated, tightly covered. Reheat it, covered, in a 350ºF oven for 20 to 25 minutes, or until hot.

Variations:

* Add 2 tablespoons chopped dried mushrooms, and ½ pound sautéed mushrooms, or a combination of white and wild mushrooms at the onset of the cooking time.
* Add ½ cup crumbled gorgonzola cheese along with the Parmesan.
* Add ½ pound fresh asparagus, cut into 1-inch sections, to the slow cooker 1½ hours into the cooking time.
* Add 1 cup butternut squash, peeled and cut into ½-inch cubes, to the slow cooker at the onset of the cooking time.
* Substitute beef stock for the chicken stock, and substitute red wine for the white wine.
* Add 2 tablespoons tomato paste to the slow cooker, and add 2 tablespoons chopped fresh oregano and 1 tablespoon chopped fresh basil.
* Substitute seafood stock for the chicken stock, and stir 1 cup diced cooked lobster or shrimp into the slow cooker at the end of the cooking time.

Risotto is one of Milan's contributions to Italian cuisine, and legend has it that it originated in the sixteenth century. True risotto *alla milanese* is made with saffron, which perfumes the rice and creates a pale yellow dish. Today, almost any creamy rice dish with cheese added is called a risotto, but the authentic dish is made with Arborio rice, which, when cooked, releases a starch and creates its own sauce. The traditional dish requires constant stirring—a step happily unnecessary with the slow cooker version.

Chapter 5

Fish and Seafood

Secondi

With the exception of the northern border, Italy is surrounded by water so it is not surprising that almost all regions—even regions not actually on the various coasts—have special fish dishes. Fish and seafood is glorified in Italian cuisine, and one of the most sensual sights in the world is visiting the famed Mercato del Pesce, or the Fish Market, in Venice. Located along the Grand Canal just behind the Rialto Bridge, it is dubbed as Cuore della Città, or the heart of the city. Through the arched entrances is an array of fish and seafood in all shapes, colors, and sizes.

Certainly Italian cuisine offers a wonderful collection of fish stews, but there are braised dishes too. When I first started writing slow cooker cookbooks more than a decade ago I was stymied by using fish, until I realized that to create successful fish dishes with the slow cooker I had to reverse the order of when ingredients were added. While chicken and meats are placed in the slow cooker at the onset of cooking, or soon thereafter, fish and seafood is the last ingredient to be added to these recipes due to its relatively short cooking time. Cubes of fish cook in mere minutes, while it can take cubes of beef up to 8 hours to reach tenderness. In fact, overcooking is a common mistake cooks make when handling seafood.

Another difference when cooking fish and seafood is that it does not freeze well—either before or after cooking. The reason is that when food is frozen the liquid inside the cells expand to form ice. This expansion punctures the delicate cell walls, which makes the fish mushy once thawed. So my suggestion is to double or even triple the recipe for the base *only*. Then freeze the extra portions of base. Thaw it when you come home, add the fresh fish, and within 10 minutes you'll be enjoying a delicious meal with perfectly cooked fish.

Secrets to Selection

Fish fillets or steaks should look bright, lustrous, and moist, with no signs of discoloration or drying.

Above all, do not buy any fish that actually smells fishy, indicating that it is no longer fresh or hasn't been cut or stored properly. Fresh fish has the mild, clean scent of the sea—nothing more. Look for bright, shiny colors in the fish scales, because as a fish sits, its skin becomes more pale and dull looking. Then peer into the eyes; they should be black and beady. If they're milky or sunken, the fish has been dead too long. And if the fish isn't behind glass, gently poke its flesh. If the indentation remains, the fish is old.

It's more important to use the freshest fish in the market rather than a particular species. All fin fish fall into three basic families, and you can easily substitute one species for another. Use the following table to make life at the fish counter easier.

A Guide to Fish

DESCRIPTION	SPECIES	CHARACTERISTICS
Firm, lean	black sea bass, cod family, flat fish (flounder, sole, halibut), grouper, lingcod, ocean perch, perch, pike, porgy, red snapper, smelt, striped bass, turbot, salmon, trout, drum family, tilefish	low-fat, mild to delicate flavor, firm flesh, flakes when cooked
Meaty	catfish, carp, eel, monkfish (anglerfish), orange roughy, pike, salmon, shark, sturgeon, swordfish, some tuna varieties, mahi-mahi (dolphin fish), whitefish, pompano, yellowtail	low to high fat, diverse flavors and textures, usually thick steaks or fillets
Fatty or strong-flavored	bluefish, mackerel, some tuna varieties	high fat, pronounced flavor

Fish is high in protein and low to moderate in fat, cholesterol, and sodium. A 3-ounce portion of fish has between 47 and 170 calories, depending on the species, and is an excellent source of B vitamins, iodine, phosphorus, potassium, iron, and calcium. The most important nutrient in fish may be the omega-3 fatty acids. These are the primary polyunsaturated fatty acids found in the fat and oils of fish. They lower the levels of low-density lipoproteins (LDL, the "bad" cholesterol) and raise the levels of high-density lipoproteins (HDL, the "good" cholesterol). Fatty fish that live in cold water, such as mackerel and salmon, seem to have the most omega-3 fatty acids.

Calamari Stuffed with Sausage and Raisins

The stuffing for this dish, served in many southern regions of Italy, makes the delicate squid far heartier, and it appeals to many diners who say they don't like fish. Because of its earthy nature, try serving it with Farro Pilaf (page 235).

Makes 4 to 6 servings | Prep time: 25 minutes | Minimum cook time: 2 hours in a medium slow cooker

1½ pounds large squid (about 10 to 12)

3 tablespoons olive oil, divided

¼ pound bulk sweet Italian sausage

2 shallots, minced

2 garlic cloves, minced

½ cup cooked white rice

2 tablespoons finely chopped raisins

Salt and freshly ground black pepper to taste

1 cup Herbed Tomato Sauce (page 97) or purchased marinara sauce

⅓ cup dry white wine

Toothpicks

1. Rinse squid inside and out, and clean if necessary. Chop the tentacles very finely, and set aside.

2. Heat 1 tablespoon oil in a medium skillet over medium-high heat. Crumble sausage into the skillet, and cook, breaking up lumps with a fork, for 2 minutes. Add shallots and garlic, and cook, stirring frequently, for 3 minutes, or until shallots begin to soften. Scrape mixture into a mixing bowl, and add rice, raisins, and squid tentacles. Season to taste with salt and pepper, and stir well.

3. Stuff a portion of stuffing into each squid, and close each tightly with toothpicks.

4. Heat remaining oil in the skillet over medium-high heat. Add squid, and brown on both sides, turning them gently with tongs. This may have to be done in batches. Transfer squid to the slow cooker, and add tomato sauce and wine.

5. Cook on High for 1 hour, then reduce the heat to Low, and cook for 1 to 1¹/₂ hours, or until squid are tender when pierced with the tip of a parking knife. Remove squid from the slow cooker with a slotted spoon, and discard toothpicks. Season sauce to taste with salt and pepper, and serve hot.

Note: The dish can be prepared up to 1 day in advance and refrigerated, tightly covered. Reheat it, covered, over low heat until hot, stirring occasionally.

Variation:

✳ Substitute thin fillets of sole or flounder for the squid. Fold them in half to enclose the stuffing, and pin them closed with toothpicks.

> If you can't find bulk sausage you can always find sausage links at the market, but push the sausage out of the casings before browning it. You'll think you're chewing rubber bands if the casings end up in the dish.

Calamari with Garbanzo Beans and Greens

This colorful treatment of tender squid comes from Liguria, and there's a bit of heat to it from the use of crushed red pepper flakes. The Swiss chard adds pretty color to the plate too. Serve some rice to enjoy all the sauce.

Makes 4 to 6 servings | Prep time: 25 minutes | Minimum cook time: 1¹/₂ hours in a medium slow cooker

1 large bunch Swiss chard

1½ pounds cleaned squid

¼ cup olive oil

1 medium onion, diced

2 garlic cloves, minced

1 carrot, chopped

1 (14.5-ounce) can diced tomatoes, undrained

½ cup Seafood Stock (page 25) or purchased stock

½ cup dry white wine

2 tablespoons chopped fresh parsley

1 tablespoon fresh chopped oregano or 1 teaspoon dried

½ to 1 teaspoon crushed red pepper flakes

1 (15-ounce) can garbanzo beans, drained and rinsed

Salt and freshly ground black pepper to taste

1. Bring a large pot of salted water to a boil, and have a bowl of ice water handy. Discard tough stems from Swiss chard, and cut leaves into 1-inch slices. Boil Swiss chard for 2 minutes, then drain, and plunge into ice water to stop the cooking action. Drain again, and transfer Swiss chard to the slow cooker.

2. Rinse squid inside and out, and clean if necessary. Cut bodies into rings ³/₄-inch wide, and leave tentacles whole. Set aside.

3. Heat oil in a medium skillet over medium-high heat. Add onion, garlic, and carrot, and cook, stirring frequently, for 5 minutes, or until onions softens. Add tomatoes, stock, wine, parsley, oregano, and red pepper flakes to the skillet, and bring to a boil over high heat. Pour mixture into the slow cooker.

4. Add squid to the slow cooker, and stir well. Cook on Low for 2 to 4 hours, or on High for 1 to 2 hours, or until squid is tender. If cooking on Low, raise the heat to high. Add garbanzo beans, and cook for 15 minutes, or until heated through. Season to taste with salt and pepper, and serve hot.

Note: The dish can be prepared up to 1 day in advance and refrigerated, tightly covered. Reheat it, covered, over low heat until hot, stirring occasionally.

Variation:

✳ Substitute extra-large shrimp, peeled and deveined, for the squid. The cooking time will remain the same.

The actual homeland of Swiss chard isn't in Switzerland but in the Mediterranean region. The Greek philosopher Aristotle wrote about chard in the fourth century BCE; both the ancient Greeks and Romans praised chard for its medicinal properties. Chard got its common name from another Mediterranean vegetable, cardoon, a celery-like plant with thick stalks that resemble those of chard.

Tomato-Braised Tuna

Tuna is caught in the waters off Sicily, and in this recipe the gentle heat of the slow cooker glorifies this meaty fish while keeping it fairly rare. If you have any left over, serve it over pasta the next day, breaking the fish up into pieces.

Makes 4 to 6 servings | Prep time: 15 minutes | Minimum cook time: 2 hours in a medium slow cooker

1 (1½ to 2-pound) tuna fillet in one thick slice

¼ cup olive oil, divided

½ small red onion, chopped

3 garlic cloves, minced

1½ cups Herbed Tomato Sauce (page 97) or purchased marinara sauce

½ cup dry white wine

3 tablespoons capers, drained and rinsed

2 tablespoons chopped fresh parsley

1 bay leaf

Salt and freshly ground black pepper to taste

1. Soak tuna in cold salted water for 10 minutes. Pat dry with paper towels.

2. Heat 2 tablespoons oil in a large skillet over medium-high heat. Add onion and garlic, and cook, stirring frequently, for 3 minutes, or until onion is translucent. Scrape mixture into the slow cooker. Add tomato sauce, wine, capers, parsley, and bay leaf to the slow cooker, and stir well. Cook on High for 1 hour.

3. Heat remaining oil in the skillet over medium-high heat. Add tuna, and brown well on both sides. Add tuna to the slow cooker, and cook on High for an additional 1 to 1½ hours, or until tuna is cooked but still rare in the center. Remove and discard bay leaf, season to taste with salt and pepper, and serve hot.

Note: The dish should be cooked just prior to serving.

Variation:
✳ Substitute salmon or swordfish for the tuna.

> Soaking the tuna in water removes a lot of its remaining blood, so that the finished dish is lighter in color and not bright red. The same treatment can be used on other dark fish, such as mackerel or bluefish.

Fish with Tomatoes and Fennel

This is one of my favorite fish dishes for any season. Fish fillets are cooked on top of a delicious and aromatic bed of vegetables scented with orange. All the vegetables you need are right in the dish, so serve some rice with it.

Makes 4 to 6 servings | Prep time: 15 minutes | Minimum cook time: 3 hours in a medium slow cooker

2 medium fennel bulbs

¼ cup olive oil

1 large onion, thinly sliced

2 garlic cloves, minced

1 (28-ounce) can diced tomatoes, drained

½ cup dry white wine

1 tablespoon grated orange zest

½ cup freshly squeezed orange juice

1 tablespoon fennel seeds, crushed

2 pounds thick firm-fleshed white fish fillets such as cod or halibut, cut into serving-sized pieces

Salt and freshly ground black pepper to taste

1. Discard stalks from fennel, and save for another use. Rinse fennel, cut in half lengthwise, and discard core and top layer of flesh. Slice fennel thinly, and set aside.

2. Heat oil in a large skillet over medium-high heat. Add onion and garlic, and cook, stirring frequently, for 3 minutes, or until onion is translucent. Add fennel and cook for an additional 2 minutes. Scrape mixture into the slow cooker.

3. Add tomatoes, wine, orange zest, orange juice, and fennel seeds to the slow cooker, and stir well. Cook on Low for 5 to 7 hours or on High for 2½ to 3 hours, or until fennel is crisp-tender.

4. If cooking on Low, raise the heat to High. Season fish with salt and pepper, and place it on top of vegetables. Cook for 30 to 45 minutes, or until fish is cooked through and flakes easily. Season to taste with salt and pepper, and serve hot.

Note: The vegetable mixture can be cooked up to 2 days in advance and refrigerated, tightly covered. Reheat it in a microwave oven or over low heat, and return it to the slow cooker. The fish should be cooked just prior to serving.

Variation:

✳ Substitute jumbo shrimp for the fish, and reduce the cooking time by 10 to 15 minutes.

While this is hardly Italian, when I cook fennel I frequently include a few pods of star anise, the Chinese spice that is one of the components of five-spice powder. Fennel, even with the addition of crushed fennel seeds, loses much of its anise flavor when it's braised, and the star anise pods add it back.

Monkfish with Cabbage, Pancetta, and Rosemary

Monkfish, sometimes called "poor man's lobster" because its sweet flavor and texture are similar to the prized crustacean, is popular in the regions bordering the Adriatic Sea, including the Veneto and Abruzzo. This preparation, scented with rosemary, and hearty with pancetta, is wonderful served with steamed potatoes.

Makes 4 to 6 servings | *Prep time: 25 minutes* | *Minimum cook time: 2 hours in a medium slow cooker*

½ small (1½-pound) head Savoy or green cabbage

¼ pound pancetta, diced

2 pounds monkfish fillets, trimmed and cut into serving pieces

2 garlic cloves, minced

1 cup Seafood Stock (page 25) or purchased stock

2 tablespoons chopped fresh rosemary or 2 teaspoons dried

1 tablespoon chopped fresh parsley

2 teaspoons grated lemon zest

Salt and freshly ground black pepper to taste

2 tablespoons unsalted butter

1. Rinse and core cabbage. Cut into wedges and then shred cabbage. Bring a large pot of salted water to a boil. Add cabbage and boil for 4 minutes. Drain cabbage and place it in the slow cooker.

2. Cook pancetta in a heavy skillet over medium heat for 5 to 7 minutes, or until crisp. Remove pancetta from the skillet with a slotted spoon, and place it in the slow cooker. Raise the heat to high, and sear monkfish in the fat on all sides, turning the pieces gently with tongs, until browned. Refrigerate monkfish.

3. Add garlic, stock, rosemary, parsley, and lemon zest to the slow cooker, and stir well. Cook on Low for 3 to 4 hours or on High for 1½ to 2 hours, or until cabbage is almost tender.

4. If cooking on Low, raise the heat to High. Season monkfish with salt and pepper, and place it on top of vegetables. Cook monkfish for 30 to 45 minutes, or until it is cooked through. Remove monkfish from the slow cooker, and keep it warm. Add butter to cabbage, and stir to melt butter. Season to taste with salt and pepper. To serve, mound equal-size portions of cabbage on each plate. Slice monkfish into medallions, and arrange on top of cabbage.

Note: The vegetable mixture can be cooked up to 2 days in advance and refrigerated, tightly covered. Reheat it in a microwave oven or over low heat, and return it to the slow cooker. The fish should be cooked just prior to serving.

Variation:
* Substitute thick fillets of halibut or cod, and the cooking time will remain the same.

> Cabbage is clearly one of the sturdier vegetables, and it will keep refrigerated for up to six weeks if not cut. Looser heads like Savoy and Napa cabbage should be used within three weeks. Do not wash it before storing it because moisture will bring on decay.

Poached Fish with Vegetables and Herbs

This is a subtle dish from Apulia, and it's sort of a cross between a braise and a stew. There is some liquid, so I usually serve it in a shallow soup bowl, but you also need a knife and fork because the fish is in large pieces.

Makes 4 to 6 servings | Prep time: 25 minutes | Minimum cook time: 2 hours in a medium slow cooker

1 pound thick firm-fleshed white fish fillets, such as cod, halibut, or sea bass, cut into serving pieces

¼ cup olive oil, divided

Salt and freshly ground black pepper to taste

1 large sweet onion, like Vidalia or Bermuda, halved and thinly sliced

2 celery ribs, sliced

½ small fennel bulb, trimmed, cored, and thinly sliced

2 cups Seafood Stock (page 25) or purchased stock

1 (14.5-ounce) can diced tomatoes, undrained

½ cup dry white wine

½ cup chopped fresh parsley, divided

2 tablespoons chopped fresh oregano or 2 teaspoons dried

2 teaspoons grated lemon zest

1 bay leaf

½ pound large shrimp, peeled and deveined

1 dozen littleneck clams, well scrubbed

1. Rinse fish and pat dry with paper towels. Rub fish with 2 tablespoons olive oil, and sprinkle with salt and pepper. Refrigerate, tightly covered with plastic wrap.

2. Heat oil in a large skillet over medium-high heat. Add onion, celery, and fennel, and cook, stirring frequently, for 3 minutes, or until onion is translucent. Scrape mixture into the slow cooker.

3. Add stock, tomatoes, wine, 3 tablespoons parsley, oregano, lemon zest, and bay leaf to the slow cooker, and stir well. Cook on Low for 4 to 5 hours or on High for 2 to 2½ hours, or until vegetables are crisp-tender.

4. If cooking on Low, raise the heat to High. Add fish, shrimp, and clams, and cook for 45 minutes to 1 hour, or until fish is cooked through and flakes easily. Remove and discard bay leaf, and season to taste with salt and pepper. Serve hot, sprinkling each serving with remaining parsley.

Note: The vegetable mixture can be cooked up to 2 days in advance and refrigerated, tightly covered. Reheat it in a microwave oven or over low heat, and return it to the slow cooker. The fish should be cooked just prior to serving.

Variation:

* Substitute red wine for the white wine, and add 2 tablespoons tomato paste to the slow cooker.

The laurel tree, native to Asia Minor, from which the bay leaf comes, was very important in both ancient Greece and Rome. The laurel can be found as a central component in many ancient mythologies that glorify the tree as a symbol of honor. In the Elizabethan era, some people believed pinning bay leaves to one's pillow on the eve of St. Valentine's Day would bring the image of your future spouse to your dream.

Fish Stew with Potatoes and Greens

Every cuisine that borders a body of water has a wonderful selection of fish stews that were created by the fishermen with whatever they caught in the nets that day. This hearty stew is topped with a dollop of a garlicky mayonnaise.

Makes 4 to 6 servings as an entrée and 6 to 8 servings as a primi | *Prep time: 20 minutes* | *Minimum cook time: 3½ hours in a medium slow cooker*

1½ pounds halibut, cod, monkfish, snapper, sea bass, or any firm-fleshed white fish

2 tablespoons olive oil

2 medium onions, diced

7 garlic cloves, minced, divided

4 cups Seafood Stock (page 25) or purchased stock

½ cup dry white wine

2 tablespoons freshly squeezed lemon juice

1 pound redskin potatoes, scrubbed and cut into ¾-inch dice

2 tablespoons chopped fresh parsley

1 tablespoon fresh thyme or ½ teaspoon dried

1 bay leaf

½ pound escarole

Salt and freshly ground black pepper to taste

½ cup mayonnaise

1 teaspoon grated lemon zest

1. Rinse fish and pat dry with paper towels. Remove and discard any skin or bones. Cut fish into 1-inch cubes. Refrigerate fish until ready to use, tightly covered with plastic wrap.

2. Heat oil in a small skillet over medium-high heat. Add onion and 3 garlic cloves, and cook, stirring frequently, for 3 minutes, or until onion is translucent. Scrape the mixture into the slow cooker.

3. Add stock, wine, lemon juice, potatoes, parsley, thyme, and bay leaf to the slow cooker, and stir well. Cook on Low for 6 to 8 hours or on High for 3 to 4 hours, or until potatoes are tender.

4. While stew cooks, prepare escarole. Rinse leaves, and discard stems. Cut leaves crosswise into ½-inch slices. Make sauce by combining mayonnaise, lemon zest, and remaining garlic. Refrigerate until ready to serve.

5. If cooking on Low, raise the heat to High. Add fish and escarole. Cook for 40 to 55 minutes, or until fish is just cooked through and flakes easily. Remove and discard bay leaf, season to taste with salt and pepper, and serve hot. Pass sauce separately.

Note: The soup can be prepared up to 3 days in advance and refrigerated, tightly covered. Reheat it, covered, over low heat, stirring occasionally.

Variations:

* Substitute Swiss chard or kale for the escarole.
* Substitute boneless, skinless chicken for the fish, and substitute chicken stock for the fish stock. Add the chicken to the slow cooker at the onset of the cooking time.

A vegetable peeler and a pair of tweezers are the best ways to get rid of those pesky little bones in fish fillets. Run a peeler down the center of the fillet, starting at the tail end. It will catch the larger pin bones, and with a twist of your wrist, you can pull them out. For finer bones, use your fingers to rub the flesh lightly and then pull out the bones with the tweezers.

Seafood Stew with Sausage

This stew is a hearty and flavorful dish, with both sausage and pancetta enlivening the flavor. Serve it with some crusty bread to soak up the delicious broth.

Makes 4 to 6 servings as an entrée and 6 to 8 servings as a primi | Prep time: 20 minutes | Minimum cook time: 3^1/$_2$ hours in a medium slow cooker

½ pound thick cod fillet

½ pound swordfish fillet

½ pound bay scallops

2 juice oranges, washed

¼ pound pancetta or bacon, diced

1 medium onion, diced

1 carrot, sliced

1 celery rib, sliced

3 garlic cloves, minced

½ pound luganega or other fresh pork sausage, removed from casings if necessary

1 (14.5-ounce) can diced tomatoes, undrained

½ cup dry white wine

3 cups Seafood Stock (page 25) or purchased stock

3 tablespoons chopped fresh basil or 1 teaspoon dried

2 tablespoons chopped fresh parsley

1 tablespoon fresh thyme or ½ teaspoon dried

1 bay leaf

Salt and freshly ground black pepper to taste

1. Rinse fish and pat dry with paper towels. Remove and discard any skin or bones. Cut fish into 1-inch cubes. Refrigerate fish and scallops until ready to use, tightly covered with plastic wrap. Grate off zest, and then squeeze oranges for juice. Set aside.

2. Cook pancetta in a heavy skillet over medium-high heat for 4 to 5 minutes, or until browned. Remove pancetta from the pan with a slotted spoon, and transfer it to the slow cooker. Discard all but 2 tablespoons grease.

3. Add onion, carrot, celery, garlic, and luganega to the skillet. Cook, stirring frequently, for 3 minutes, or until onion is translucent. Scrape mixture into the slow cooker.

4. Add tomatoes, orange zest, orange juice, wine, stock, basil, parsley, thyme, and bay leaf to the slow cooker, and stir well. Cook on Low for 6 to 8 hours or on High for 3 to 4 hours, or until vegetables are soft.

5. If cooking on Low, raise the heat to High. Add fish, and cook for 30 to 50 minutes, or until fish is cooked through and flakes easily. Remove and discard bay leaf, season to taste with salt and pepper, and serve hot.

Note: The stew can be prepared up to 1 day in advance and refrigerated, tightly covered. Reheat it, covered, over low heat, stirring occasionally.

Variation:

✳ Substitute boneless, skinless chicken for the fish and substitute chicken stock for the fish stock. Add the chicken to the slow cooker at the onset of the cooking time.

Whenever zest from a citrus fruit is being added to a dish, I always suggest washing the fruit with mild soap and water before grating the zest off. Many citrus growers spray with pesticides, and the residue remains on the fruit. Also, some fruit is lightly waxed before shipment to make it more transportable.

Hearty Shellfish Stew

This is the sort of fish stew that has become known as Cioppino in San Franciso and other American cities. It's made with red wine and lots of tomatoes. Serve a red wine with it too.

Makes 4 to 6 servings as an entrée and 6 to 8 servings as a primi | Prep time: 25 minutes | Minimum cook time: 3 hours in a medium slow cooker

¾ pound thick firm-fleshed fish fillet, such as cod, swordfish, or halibut

¾ pound sea scallops

½ pound extra-large (16 to 20 per pound) shrimp

1 dozen mussels, scrubbed and debearded

3 tablespoons olive oil

2 medium onions, diced

1 red bell pepper, seeds and ribs removed, and finely chopped

2 celery ribs, diced

3 garlic cloves, minced

2 tablespoons chopped fresh oregano or 2 teaspoons dried

2 teaspoons fresh thyme or ¼ teaspoon dried

1 (28-ounce) can diced tomatoes, undrained

1½ cups dry red wine

1 cup Seafood Stock (page 25) or purchased stock

2 tablespoons tomato paste

1 bay leaf

¼ cup chopped fresh parsley

3 tablespoons chopped fresh basil or 2 teaspoons dried

Salt and freshly ground black pepper to taste

1. Rinse fish and pat dry with paper towels. Remove and discard any skin or bones. Cut fish into 1-inch cubes.

Cut scallops in half. Peel and devein shrimp. Refrigerate all seafood until ready to use, tightly covered with plastic wrap.

2. Heat olive oil in a medium skillet over medium-high heat. Add onions, red bell pepper, celery, garlic, oregano, and thyme. Cook, stirring frequently, for 3 minutes, or until onions are translucent. Scrape mixture into the slow cooker.

3. Add tomatoes, wine, stock, tomato paste, and bay leaf to the slow cooker, and stir well to dissolve tomato paste. Cook on Low for 5 to 7 hours or on High for 2½ to 3 hours, or until vegetables are almost tender.

4. If cooking on Low, raise the heat to High. Add seafood, parsley, and basil. Cook for 30 to 45 minutes, or until fish is cooked through. Remove and discard bay leaf, season to taste with salt and pepper, and serve hot.

Note: The stew can be prepared up to 1 day in advance and refrigerated, tightly covered. Reheat it, covered, over low heat, stirring occasionally.

Variation:

❊ Substitute squid for the sea scallops. Clean them, slice the bodies into ½-inch rings, and keep the tentacles whole.

Do not equate the words "fresh shrimp" with shrimp that have never been frozen. Truth be told, you probably will be unable to find never-frozen shrimp fresh from the ocean these days unless you have a shrimper friend or net it yourself. This is not necessarily a bad thing. Nowadays, shrimp is harvested, cleaned, and flash frozen on the boats before they ever reach the shore. But if you plan to freeze shrimp, ask the fishmonger to sell you some still frozen rather than thawed in the case.

Mussel Stew with Beans

From Tuscany, this blend of briny mussels, white beans, tomatoes, and lots of garlic makes an ideal supper with some crusty bread and a green salad.

Yield: 4 to 6 servings as an entrée and 6 to 8 servings as a primi | Prep time: 20 minutes | Minimum cook time: 3¹/₂ hours in a large slow cooker

2 tablespoons olive oil

1 large onion, diced

2 garlic cloves, minced

1 large carrot, diced

2 celery ribs, diced

5 cups Seafood Stock (page 25) or purchased stock

1 (14.5-ounce) can diced tomatoes, undrained

1 cup dry white wine

3 tablespoons chopped fresh parsley

1 teaspoon fresh thyme or pinch dried

3 pounds live mussels

2 (15-ounce) cans cannellini beans, rinsed and drained

Salt and freshly ground black pepper to taste

1. Heat oil in a skillet over medium-high heat. Add onion, garlic, carrot, and celery. Cook, stirring frequently, for 3 minutes, or until onion is translucent. Scrape mixture into the slow cooker.

2. Add stock, tomatoes, wine, parsley, and thyme to the slow cooker, and stir well. Cook on Low for 3 to 5 hours, or on High for 1¹/₂ to 2 hours, or until vegetables are crisp-tender.

3. While base cooks, clean mussels by scrubbing them well with a brush under cold water; discard any that do not shut tightly. Scrape off any barnacles with a knife. If beard is still attached, remove it by pulling it from tip to hinge, or by pulling and cutting it off with knife. Set aside.

4. If cooking on Low, raise the heat to High. Add mussels and beans to the slow cooker. Cook on High for 1¹/₂ to 2 hours, or until mussels open. Shake the slow cooker a few times, without opening it, to redistribute mussels. Discard any mussels that did not open, and remove the pan from the heat.

5. Season broth to taste with salt and pepper. To serve, place mussels in shallow bowls and ladle broth and vegetables on top. Serve with soup spoons as well as seafood forks.

Note: The stew base can be prepared up to 2 days in advance and refrigerated, tightly covered. Reheat it, covered, over low heat, stirring frequently until it comes to a boil, and then add mussels.

Variation:

✳ Substitute 1¹/₄ pounds thick white firm-fleshed fish fillets, rinsed and cut into 1-inch cubes, for the mussels. Cook the fish on High for 20 to 40 minutes, or until it is cooked through and flakes easily.

Cultured mussels have been around since the twelfth century. A ship-wrecked sailor off the coast of France placed poles with netting in the water to catch fish. When he checked the nets, he noticed that mussels had attached themselves to the poles. This has become known today as the Bouchot method, and it is still used extensively.

Chapter 6

Poultry

Secondi

*I*f you're like most North Americans, it's a safe bet that roughly three nights a week you're having some form of chicken for dinner. Chicken is the food that dominates the center of our plates, with per capita consumption now topping 90 pounds. That figure has more than doubled since 1970, and beef consumption has declined as a result.

Poultry does not share this place of honor in Italian homes. The country ranks about twenty countries behind the United States in poultry popularity. However, most regions have some wonderful chicken dishes, and those are the recipes you'll find in this chapter. Many of the chickens are cooked in red wine and can be served with it at the table too. The "white wine with white meat" approach is not part of Italian cuisine. At the end of the chapter are a few recipes for turkey, which is not a traditional meat in Italy, and duck too.

Safety First

Poultry should always be rinsed under cold running water after being taken out of the package. If it's going to be pre-browned under the broiler or in a skillet on the stove, pat the pieces dry with paper towels and then wash your hands. Chicken often contains salmonella, a naturally occurring bacterium that is killed by cooking, but you don't want to transfer this bacterium to other foods. That's why cooked chicken should never be placed on a platter that held it raw. For the same reason, if you are prepping ingredients in the evening to cook the next day in the slow cooker, never refrigerate the chicken with other ingredients, and never pre-brown chicken and then refrigerate it again.

For the sake of food safety, it's best not to cook a whole chicken in the slow cooker, because the low heat might keep the meat of a whole bird in the bacterial danger zone of 40°F to 140°F for more than two hours. For these recipes calling for whole chickens, I advocate using thighs, legs, and breasts, which can be cut in half. They're bigger than the other pieces and they fit more neatly in the slow cooker if cut. Save the wings separately for making baked or grilled wings for a picnic or snack; there's not enough meat on them to justify taking up room in the slow cooker.

Chicken with Spring Vegetables and Pancetta

Chicken is inherently delicate, and that quality is conveyed beautifully in this light dish with accents of pearl onion and peas.

Makes 4 to 6 servings | Prep time: 20 minutes | Minimum cook time: 3¼ hours in a medium slow cooker

1 (3- to 4-pound) chicken, cut into serving pieces, or 6 chicken pieces of your choice

1 tablespoon olive oil

¾ cup diced pancetta

2 shallots, minced

2 garlic cloves, minced (optional)

2 cups Chicken Stock (page 19) or purchased stock

3 tablespoons chopped fresh parsley

1 tablespoon fresh chopped rosemary or 1 teaspoon dried

1 bay leaf

1 (10-ounce) package frozen pearl onions, thawed

1 (10-ounce) package frozen peas, thawed

Salt and freshly ground black pepper to taste

1. Preheat the oven broiler, and line a broiler pan with heavy-duty aluminum foil. Rinse chicken and pat dry with paper towels. Broil chicken pieces for 3 minutes per side, or until browned. Transfer chicken pieces to the slow cooker, skin side down.

2. Heat oil in a medium skillet over medium-high heat. Add pancetta, and cook, stirring frequently, for 3 to 5 minutes, or until pancetta is brown. Remove pancetta from the skillet with a slotted spoon, and place it in the slow cooker. Add shallots and garlic, if using, to the skillet, and cook, stirring frequently, for 3 minutes, or until shallots are translucent. Scrape mixture into the slow cooker.

2. Add stock, parsley, rosemary, and bay leaf to the slow cooker, and stir well. Cook on Low for 5 to 7 hours or on High for 2½ to 3 hours, or until chicken is almost cooked through.

3. If cooking on Low, raise the heat to High. Add onions and peas, and cook for 45 to 55 minutes, or until chicken is cooked through, tender, and no longer pink, and mixture is bubbling. Remove and discard bay leaf, season to taste with salt and pepper, and serve hot.

Note: The dish can be prepared up to 2 days in advance and refrigerated, tightly covered. Reheat it, covered, in a 350°F oven for 20 to 25 minutes, or until hot.

Variation:

＊ Substitute frozen artichoke hearts for the peas.

> While pancetta is now available in just about every North American supermarket, if you can't find it, you can always substitute bacon. Try to find a bacon that is not heavily smoked or cured.

Chicken with Peppers in Red Wine

This dish of chicken cooked with sweet bell peppers and herbs in red wine comes from Umbria. A dish like Farro Pilaf (page 235) stands up to the heartiness of the flavors.

Makes 4 to 6 servings | Prep time: 20 minutes | Minimum cook time: 3 hours in a medium slow cooker

1 (3- to 4-pound) chicken, cut into serving pieces, or 6 chicken pieces of your choice

3 tablespoons olive oil

2 medium onions, diced

3 garlic cloves, minced

1 carrot, diced

1 celery rib, diced

3 red bell peppers, seeds and ribs removed, and cut into thin strips

1½ cups dry red wine

1 (14.5-ounce) can diced tomatoes, undrained

3 tablespoons chopped fresh parsley

2 tablespoons chopped fresh oregano or 2 teaspoons dried

1 tablespoon tomato paste

Salt and freshly ground black pepper to taste

1. Preheat the oven broiler, and line a broiler pan with heavy-duty aluminum foil. Rinse chicken and pat dry with paper towels. Broil chicken pieces for 3 minutes per side, or until browned. Transfer chicken pieces to the slow cooker, skin side down.

2. Heat oil in a large skillet over medium-high heat. Add onions, garlic, carrot, celery, and red bell peppers. Cook, stirring frequently, for 5 minutes, or until peppers begin to soften. Scrape mixture into the slow cooker.

3. Add wine, tomatoes, parsley, oregano, and tomato paste to the slow cooker, and stir well to dissolve tomato paste. Cook on Low for 6 to 8 hours or on High for 3 to 4 hours, or until chicken is cooked through, tender, and no longer pink. Season to taste with salt and pepper, and serve hot.

Note: The dish can be prepared up to 2 days in advance and refrigerated, tightly covered. Reheat it, covered, in a 350°F oven for 20 to 25 minutes, or until hot.

Variations:

* Substitute dry white wine for the red wine, and add 1 tablespoon grated orange zest.

* Cook ¼ pound diced pancetta in a skillet over medium-high heat for 4 to 5 minutes, or until browned. Add it to the slow cooker along with the chicken.

> When cooking with wine or any other acid such as lemon juice, it's important to use a stainless-steel or coated steel pan rather than aluminum. When mixed with the wine or acid, an aluminum pan can impart a metallic taste to the dish.

Chicken with Mushrooms

Cacciatore is Italian for "hunter's style," and since Italians in all regions are hunters this dish is almost a national one. A number of foods from chicken to beef to veal use cacciatore as a handle, but all it means is that the dish is cooked with tomatoes, onions, pancetta, and mushrooms. The rest of the ingredients are up to the cook.

Makes 4 to 6 servings | Prep time: 20 minutes | Minimum cook time: 3 hours in a medium slow cooker

1 (3- to 4-pound) chicken, cut into serving pieces, or 6 chicken pieces of your choice

¼ cup olive oil

2 large onions, halved and thinly sliced

2 garlic cloves, minced

1 pound cremini mushrooms, wiped with a damp paper towel, trimmed, and sliced

1 (28-ounce) can diced tomatoes, undrained

½ cup dry white wine

1 tablespoon fresh thyme or ½ teaspoon dried

1 tablespoon chopped fresh sage or 1 teaspoon dried

1 tablespoon chopped fresh rosemary or 1 teaspoon dried

Salt and freshly ground black pepper to taste

1. Preheat the oven broiler, and line a broiler pan with heavy-duty aluminum foil. Rinse chicken and pat dry with paper towels. Broil chicken pieces for 3 minutes per side, or until browned. Transfer chicken pieces to the slow cooker, skin side down.

2. Heat oil in a large skillet over medium-high heat. Add onions, garlic, and mushrooms, and cook, stirring frequently, for 5 minutes, or until mushrooms begin to soften. Scrape mixture into the slow cooker.

3. Add tomatoes, wine, thyme, sage, and rosemary to the slow cooker, and stir well. Cook on Low for 6 to 8 hours or on High for 3 to 4 hours, or until chicken is cooked through, tender, and no longer pink. Season to taste with salt and pepper, and serve hot.

Note: The dish can be prepared up to 2 days in advance and refrigerated, tightly covered. Reheat it, covered, in a 350°F oven for 20 to 25 minutes, or until hot.

Variations:

＊ Substitute 4 to 6 (4 to 6-ounce) boneless pork chops for the chicken.

＊ Add ½ cup chopped dried porcini mushrooms to the slow cooker.

> Most of the mushrooms we find in supermarkets are the same species, *Agaricus bisporus*. What makes the difference is their age. White button mushrooms are the youngest, cremini are in the middle, and portobello is what we call them when they're big and old.

Chicken with Peppers and Olives

Both oranges and olives grow all over Sicily, and those are joined by colorful bell peppers in this exuberant dish that is perfect in any season of the year. Serve it with rice.

Makes 4 to 6 servings | Prep time: 20 minutes | Minimum cook time: 3 hours in a medium slow cooker

1 (3- to 4-pound) chicken, cut into serving pieces, or 6 chicken pieces of your choice

¼ cup olive oil

1 large onion, diced

2 garlic cloves, minced

1 green bell pepper, seeds and ribs removed, and diced

1 red bell pepper, seeds and ribs removed, and diced

½ cup freshly squeezed orange juice

½ cup Chicken Stock (page 19) or purchased stock

½ cup dry white wine

1 (14.5-ounce) can diced tomatoes, undrained

2 tablespoons chopped fresh parsley

1 tablespoon fresh thyme or ¼ teaspoon dried

1 tablespoon fresh chopped rosemary or 1 teaspoon dried

1 tablespoon grated orange zest

2 bay leaves

½ cup pitted oil-cured black olives

Salt and freshly ground black pepper to taste

1. Preheat the oven broiler, and line a broiler pan with heavy-duty aluminum foil. Rinse chicken and pat dry with paper towels. Broil chicken pieces for 3 minutes per side, or until browned. Transfer chicken pieces to the slow cooker, skin side down.

2. Heat oil in a large skillet over medium-high heat. Add onion, garlic, green bell pepper, and red bell pepper. Cook, stirring frequently, for 3 minutes, or until onion is translucent. Scrape mixture into the slow cooker.

3. Add orange juice, stock, wine, tomatoes, parsley, thyme, rosemary, orange zest, bay leaves, and olives to the slow cooker, and stir well. Cook chicken on Low for 6 to 8 hours or on High for 3 to 4 hours, or until chicken is cooked through and no longer pink. Remove and discard bay leaves, season to taste with salt and pepper, and serve hot.

Note: The dish can be prepared up to 2 days in advance and refrigerated, tightly covered. Reheat it, covered, in a 350°F oven for 20 to 25 minutes, or until hot.

Variation:

* Substitute cubes of veal for the chicken, and the cooking time will remain the same.

Crispy skin doesn't happen when you're cooking chicken in the slow cooker. That's just a fact. While the chicken is browned for all of these recipes so that the skin looks appealing and not pasty white, if you want crisp skin, place the pieces under the oven broiler, 8 inches beneath the element, for 3 to 5 minutes, and the skin will become crisp.

Chicken with Prosciutto "Roman-Style"

Chicken is less popular in southern Italy than it is in the northern regions because lamb and pork are so available there. This dish comes from Lazio, and it joins bits of salty prosciutto with herbs in a white wine sauce with tomatoes. Serve it with rice.

Makes 4 to 6 servings | Prep time: 15 minutes | Minimum cook time: 3 hours in a medium slow cooker

1 (3- to 4-pound) chicken, cut into serving pieces, or 6 chicken pieces of your choice

2 tablespoons olive oil

¼ pound prosciutto, cut into small julienne

1 shallot, minced

3 garlic cloves, minced

1 (14.5-ounce) can tomatoes, undrained

⅔ cup dry white wine

½ cup Chicken Stock (page 19) or purchased stock

2 tablespoons chopped fresh marjoram or 2 teaspoons dried

Salt and freshly ground black pepper to taste

1. Preheat the oven broiler, and line a broiler pan with heavy-duty aluminum foil. Rinse chicken and pat dry with paper towels. Broil chicken pieces for 3 minutes per side, or until browned. Transfer chicken pieces to the slow cooker, skin side down.

2. Heat oil in a small skillet over medium-high heat. Add prosciutto, shallot, and garlic, and cook, stirring frequently, for 3 minutes, or until shallot is translucent. Scrape mixture into the slow cooker.

3. Add tomatoes, wine, stock, and marjoram to the slow cooker, and stir well. Cook on Low for 6 to 8 hours or on High for 3 to 4 hours, or until chicken is cooked through, tender, and no longer pink. Season to taste with salt and pepper, and serve hot.

Note: The dish can be prepared up to 2 days in advance and refrigerated, tightly covered. Reheat it, covered, in a 350°F oven for 20 to 25 minutes, or until hot.

Variation:

＊ Substitute cubes of boneless pork loin or pork shoulder for the chicken, and the cooking time will remain the same.

> Just four ounces of chicken provides more than two-thirds of your protein needs for the day, and that's for only 223 calories. Another health bonus is that the fat in chicken is less saturated than the fat in beef—discounting the skin. One of the other major nutritional contributions of chicken is that the same size serving contains more than 100 percent of the daily value for tryptophan. Tryptophan is one of the 10 essential amino acids we have to eat daily.

Chicken with Potatoes and Olives

The combination of bell peppers with olives is characteristic of the cooking from Syracuse, and the salty capers and point of vinegar makes this a simultaneously light and vibrant dish.

Makes 4 to 6 servings | *Prep time: 20 minutes* | *Minimum cook time: 3¹/₄ hours in a medium slow cooker*

1 (3- to 4-pound) chicken, cut into serving pieces, or 6 chicken pieces of your choice

¼ cup olive oil

1 large red onion, halved and thinly sliced

2 garlic cloves, minced

2 celery ribs, sliced

1 red bell pepper, seeds and ribs removed, and thinly sliced

1 orange bell pepper, seeds and ribs removed, and thinly sliced

1 pound redskin potatoes, scrubbed and cut into 1-inch cubes

1 (14.5-ounce) can diced tomatoes, undrained

1½ cups Chicken Stock (page 19) or purchased stock

1 tablespoon fresh thyme or ½ teaspoon dried

½ cup sliced brine-cured green olives, preferably Sicilian

2 tablespoons capers, drained and rinsed

2 tablespoons cider vinegar

Salt and freshly ground black pepper to taste

1. Preheat the oven broiler, and line a broiler pan with heavy-duty aluminum foil. Rinse chicken and pat dry with paper towels. Broil chicken pieces for 3 minutes per side, or until browned. Transfer chicken pieces to the slow cooker, skin side down.

2. Heat oil in a large skillet over medium-high heat. Add onion, garlic, celery, red bell pepper, and orange bell pepper. Cook, stirring frequently, for 3 minutes, or until onion is translucent. Scrape mixture into the slow cooker.

3. Add potatoes, tomatoes, stock, thyme, olives, capers, and vinegar to the slow cooker, and stir well. Cook on Low for 6 to 8 hours or on High for 3 to 4 hours, or until chicken is cooked through, tender, and no longer pink. Season to taste with salt and pepper, and serve hot.

Note: The dish can be prepared up to 2 days in advance and refrigerated, tightly covered. Reheat it, covered, in a 350°F oven for 20 to 25 minutes, or until hot.

Variation:

* Substitute cubes of pork loin for the chicken, and the cooking time will remain the same.

In the seventeenth century, King Henry IV of France's Prime Minister Sully used "a chicken in every pot" as a metaphor for the prosperity he wished for his citizens. In the 1600s, chickens were associated with luxury rather than with fast food, and they were eaten only on holidays.

Chicken Breasts with Roasted Lemon and Capers

I had this dish at Lidia's in Kansas City, the Midwest outpost of chef Lidia Bastianch's chain. I'm assuming it's from her native region of Istria. Regardless, it's just delicious.

Makes 4 to 6 servings | Prep time: 15 minutes | Minimum cook time: 2 hours in a medium slow cooker

2 lemons

⅓ cup olive oil, divided

Salt and freshly ground black pepper to taste

4 to 6 (4 to 6-ounce) boneless, skinless chicken breast halves

All-purpose flour for dredging

1 cup Chicken Stock (page 19) or purchased stock

2 tablespoons capers, drained and rinsed

3 tablespoons unsalted butter, cut into small pieces

3 tablespoons chopped fresh parsley

1. Preheat the oven to 325°F, and line a baking sheet with parchment paper. Slice lemons thinly, and discard seeds. Brush slices with 1 to 2 tablespoons oil, and sprinkle with salt. Roast lemons for 25 to 30 minutes, or until they are beginning to brown around the edges. Remove lemons from the oven, and set aside.

2. Rinse chicken and pat dry with paper towels. Trim chicken of all visible fat. Sprinkle chicken with salt and pepper, and dredge in flour, shaking off excess over the sink or a garbage can.

3. Heat remaining oil in a large skillet over medium-high heat. Brown chicken breasts on both sides, turning them gently with tongs. Transfer chicken to the slow cooker.

4. Add stock to the skillet, and bring to a boil, scraping up the brown bits clinging to the bottom of the pan. Stir in capers, and pour mixture into the slow cooker. Cook on Low for 4 to 6 hours or on High for 2 to 3 hours, or chicken cooked through, tender, and no longer pink.

5. If cooking on Low, raise the heat to High. Add butter and lemon slices, and cook for 15 to 20 minutes, or until bubbly. Season to taste with salt and pepper, and serve hot, sprinkling each serving with parsley.

Note: The dish can be prepared up to 2 days in advance and refrigerated, tightly covered. Reheat it, covered, in a 350°F oven for 20 to 25 minutes, or until hot.

Variation:

✳ Substitute thinly pounded veal for the chicken, and the cooking time will remain the same.

Recipes written for boneless, skinless chicken can always be made with whole chicken pieces with bones and skin. What must be changed, however, is the amount of braising liquid as well as the cooking time. The liquid should be increased by 40 percent, and consult a similar recipe to determine the cooking time.

Chicken with Swiss Chard

This dish from Emilia-Romagna uses the region's famed balsamic vinegar in the sauce, and it includes bright green Swiss chard for a color. Serve it with some Farro with Fennel (page 233) or some rice.

Makes 4 to 6 servings | Prep time: 20 minutes | Minimum cook time: 3 hours in a medium slow cooker

1 (3- to 4-pound) chicken, cut into serving pieces, or 6 chicken pieces of your choice

2 tablespoons olive oil

1 medium onion, diced

2 garlic cloves, minced

½ cup balsamic vinegar

1 (14.5-ounce) can diced tomatoes, undrained

¾ cup Chicken Stock (page 19) or purchased stock

¼ cup dry red wine

1 tablespoon fresh thyme or ½ teaspoon dried

2 bay leaves

¼ pound Swiss chard, stems discarded and leaves cut into ¾-inch slices

2 teaspoons cornstarch

Salt and freshly ground black pepper to taste

1. Preheat the oven broiler, and line a broiler pan with heavy-duty aluminum foil. Rinse chicken and pat dry with paper towels. Broil chicken pieces for 3 minutes per side, or until browned. Transfer chicken pieces to the slow cooker, skin side down.

2. Heat oil in a small skillet over medium-high heat. Add onion and garlic, and cook, stirring frequently, for 3 minutes, or until onion is translucent. Add vinegar, and cook until liquid is reduced by half. Scrape mixture into the slow cooker.

3. Add tomatoes, stock, wine, thyme, and bay leaves to the slow cooker, and stir well. Cook on Low for 6 hours or on High for 3 hours. Add Swiss chard, and cook for an additional 2 hours on Low or 1 hour on High, or until chicken is cooked through, tender, and no longer pink.

4. If cooking on Low, raise the heat to High. Mix cornstarch and 2 tablespoons cold water in a small cup. Stir mixture into the slow cooker. Cook for an additional 15 to 20 minutes, or until juices are bubbling and slightly thickened. Remove and discard bay leaves, season to taste with salt and pepper, and serve hot.

Note: The dish can be prepared up to 2 days in advance and refrigerated, tightly covered. Reheat it, covered, in a 350°F oven for 20 to 25 minutes, or until hot.

Variations:

* Substitute rabbit for the chicken. The cooking time will remain the same.
* Substitute kale for the Swiss chard.
* Add $1/2$ cup raisins to the slow cooker at the onset of the cooking time.

During the later part of the Middle Ages and the Renaissance era, the Italian nobility enjoyed the different varieties of vinegar as a refined drink because they believed the vinegar was a natural remedy for the plague. By the nineteenth century, balsamic vinegar was considered a precious commodity.

Chicken Breasts with Mushrooms and Marsala

Both chicken and veal are frequently paired with fortified Marsala wine, and this dish includes lots of mushrooms too. Serve it with Toasted Barley with Mushrooms (page 237) or steamed potatoes.

Makes 4 to 6 servings | Prep time: 20 minutes | Minimum cook time: 2 hours in a medium slow cooker

⅓ cup olive oil, divided

½ small onion, diced

4 garlic cloves, minced

1 pound cremini mushrooms, wiped with a damp paper towel, trimmed, and sliced

4 to 6 (4 to 6-ounce) boneless, skinless chicken breast halves

Salt and freshly ground black pepper to taste

All-purpose flour for dredging

¾ cup dry Marsala

1 cup Chicken Stock (page 19) or purchased stock

½ cup chopped fresh parsley

2 teaspoons fresh thyme or ¼ teaspoon dried

1. Heat 2 tablespoons oil in a large skillet over medium-high heat. Add onion, garlic, and mushrooms, and cook, stirring frequently, for 4 to 5 minutes, or until mushrooms begin to soften. Scrape mixture into the slow cooker.

2. Rinse chicken and pat dry with paper towels. Trim chicken of all visible fat. Sprinkle chicken with salt and pepper, and dredge in flour, shaking off excess over the sink or a garbage can.

3. Heat remaining oil in a large skillet over medium-high heat. Brown chicken breasts on both sides, turning them gently with tongs. Transfer chicken to the slow cooker.

4. Add Marsala and stock to the skillet, and bring to a boil, scraping up the brown bits clinging to the bottom of the pan. Pour liquid into the slow cooker, and stir in parsley and thyme.

5. Cook on Low for 4 to 6 hours or on High for 2 to 3 hours, or until chicken is cooked through, tender, and no longer pink. Season to taste with salt and pepper, and serve hot.

Note: The dish can be prepared up to 2 days in advance and refrigerated, tightly covered. Reheat it, covered, in a 350°F oven for 20 to 25 minutes, or until hot.

Variation:

* Substitute veal stew meat for the chicken breasts, and increase the cooking time to 6 to 8 hours on Low or 3 to 4 hours on High.

I happen to think that it's the dark meat of poultry that has the most flavor, which is why I also adore duck. If you agree, you can always substitute two chicken thighs for each breast specified in a recipe.

Herbed Chicken Breasts

I always made extra of this dish because the chicken is so good cut up and tossed with pasta on a subsequent night. It's a simple dish of chicken cooked in an herbed tomato sauce that is very quick to assemble for the slow cooker.

Makes 4 to 6 servings | Prep time: 15 minutes | Minimum cook time: 2 hours in a medium slow cooker

3 tablespoons olive oil

1 large onion, diced

3 garlic cloves, minced

½ green bell pepper, seeds and ribs removed, and chopped

4 to 6 (4 to 6-ounce) boneless, skinless chicken breast halves

1 cup Herbed Tomato Sauce (page 97) or purchased marinara sauce

½ cup dry white wine

½ cup Chicken Stock (page 19) or purchased stock

2 tablespoons chopped fresh oregano or 2 teaspoon dried

1 tablespoon fresh thyme or ½ teaspoon dried

1 tablespoon chopped fresh rosemary or 1 teaspoon dried

1 bay leaf

Salt and freshly ground black pepper to taste

1. Heat oil in a medium skillet over medium-high heat. Add onion, garlic, and green bell pepper. Cook, stirring frequently, for 3 minutes, or until onion is translucent. Scrape mixture into the slow cooker.

2. Rinse chicken and pat dry with paper towels. Trim chicken of all visible fat, and arrange chicken on top of vegetables. Combine tomato sauce, wine, stock, oregano, thyme, rosemary, and bay leaf in a small bowl. Pour mixture over chicken.

3. Cook on Low for 4 to 6 hours or on High for 2 to 3 hours, or until chicken is cooked through, tender, and no longer pink. Remove and discard bay leaf, season to taste with salt and pepper, and serve hot.

Note: The dish can be prepared up to 2 days in advance and refrigerated, tightly covered. Reheat it, covered, in a 350°F oven for 20 to 25 minutes, or until hot.

Variation:

* Substitute cubes of veal, and increase the cooking time by 2 hours on Low or 1 hour on High.

The history of marjoram and oregano are inseparable. It was believed that the Greek God Venus created the plants, and the herb was said to the favorite of Arphrodite. Oregano has been long referred to as *wild marjoram*, and, in fact, *oregano* means *marjoram* in Spanish. However, although the Mediterranean variety of oregano closely resembles and is closely related to marjoram, they are different herbs.

Turkey Tonnato

This is one of my favorite summer dishes because cooking the turkey in the slow cooker means the kitchen doesn't get hot! And the chilled turkey with tuna sauce is a delicious combination.

Makes 6 to 8 servings | Prep time: 20 minutes | Minimum cook time: 3 hours in a medium slow cooker plus 8 hours to chill

1 (2-pound) boneless, skinless turkey breast half

3 garlic cloves, peeled and cut into quarters

1½ cups Chicken Stock (page 19) or purchased stock

½ cup dry white wine

1 onion, sliced

1 carrot, sliced

4 sprigs fresh parsley

2 sprigs fresh thyme or 1 teaspoon dried

1 bay leaf

Salt and freshly ground black pepper to taste

2 (5-ounce) cans imported tuna packed in olive oil, undrained

¼ cup freshly squeezed lemon juice

2 tablespoons anchovy paste

¼ cup mayonnaise

2 tablespoons capers, drained and rinsed

1. Rinse turkey, and pat dry with paper towels. Place turkey breast between two sheets of plastic wrap. Pound with the flat side of a meat mallet or bottom of a small saucepan until it is a uniform thickness. Roll turkey breast into a shape that will fit into your slow cooker, and tie with kitchen string. Make 12 slits around turkey breast, and insert a garlic sliver in each one.

2. Place turkey breast in the slow cooker, and add stock, wine, onion, carrot, parsley, thyme, bay leaf, salt, and pepper. Cook on Low for 6 to 8 hours or on High for 3 to 4 hours, or until a thermometer inserted in the center of turkey reads 165°F. Remove turkey from the slow cooker and chill well.

3. For sauce, combine tuna, lemon juice, and anchovy paste in a food processor fitted with a steel blade or in a blender. Puree until smooth, and scrape mixture into a mixing bowl. Stir in mayonnaise and capers, and season to taste with salt and pepper.

4. To serve, remove and discard the string, and thinly slice turkey. Spoon some sauce on turkey slices, and pass remaining sauce separately.

Note: The dish and the sauce can be made up to 2 days in advance and refrigerated, tightly covered.

Variation:

* Substitute veal loin for the turkey. The cooking time will not change.

> Although there is no use for the braising liquid in this recipe, it's a richly flavored stock and it's a shame to throw it away. Freeze it and use it in place of chicken stock when cooking another recipe.

Stuffed Turkey Breast

This is a colorful dish, with a layer of bright green spinach and pink mortadella and prosciutto creating a spiral through the turkey.

Makes 6 to 8 servings | Prep time: 20 minutes | Minimum cook time: 3 hours in a medium slow cooker

1 (2-pound) boneless, skinless turkey breast half

1 (10-ounce) package frozen chopped spinach, thawed

3 tablespoons whole milk

1 large egg

½ cup breadcrumbs

Salt and freshly ground black pepper to taste

¼ pound mortadella

¼ pound prosciutto

3 garlic cloves, cut into 4 slivers each

1½ cups Chicken Stock (page 19) or purchased stock

½ cup dry white wine

1 onion, sliced

1 carrot, sliced

4 sprigs fresh parsley

2 sprigs fresh thyme or 1 teaspoon dried

1 bay leaf

1. Rinse turkey, and pat dry with paper towels. Place turkey breast between two sheets of plastic wrap. Pound with the flat side of a meat mallet or bottom of a small saucepan until it is a uniform thickness.

2. Place spinach in a colander and press with the back of a spoon to extract as much liquid as possible. Combine milk, egg, and breadcrumbs in a mixing bowl, and whisk well. Stir in spinach, and season to taste with salt and pepper.

3. Layer mortadella and prosciutto on top of turkey, and spread spinach mixture on top. Roll turkey breast into a shape that will fit into your slow cooker, and tie with kitchen string. Make 12 slits around turkey breast, and insert a garlic sliver in each one.

4. Place turkey breast in the slow cooker, and add stock, wine, onion, carrot, parsley, thyme, bay leaf, salt, and pepper. Cook on Low for 6 to 8 hours or on High for 3 to 4 hours, or until a thermometer inserted in the center of turkey reads 165°F. Remove turkey from the slow cooker. To serve, remove and discard the string, and thinly slice turkey.

Note: The dish and the sauce can be made up to 2 days in advance and refrigerated, tightly covered.

Variation:

✳ Substitute veal loin for the turkey. The cooking time will remain the same.

> Mortadella originated in Bologna, the capital of Emilia-Romagna, although the style of this ground sausage studded with cubes of pork fat changes today from region to region. In some parts of Tuscany it includes garlic, while in Lazio it's lightly smoked.

Turkey Meatloaf

The slow cooker produces wonderfully moist meatloaf, which is especially important when cooking with lean ground turkey.

Makes 4 to 6 servings | *Prep time: 15 minutes* | *Minimum cook time: 3 hours in a medium slow cooker*

2 tablespoons olive oil

1 large onion, chopped

2 garlic cloves, minced

1 celery rib, chopped

1 pound ground turkey

2 large eggs, lightly beaten

½ cup plain breadcrumbs

½ cup freshly grated Parmesan cheese

¼ cup finely chopped sun-dried tomatoes packed in oil

2 tablespoons chopped fresh parsley

2 tablespoons chopped fresh oregano or 2 teaspoons dried

Salt and freshly ground black pepper to taste

Vegetable oil spray

For serving: Herbed Tomato Sauce (page 97) or purchased marinara sauce

1. Heat oil in a medium skillet over medium-high heat. Add onion, garlic, and celery. Cook, stirring frequently, for 5 minutes, or until onion softens. Scrape mixture into a mixing bowl. Add turkey, eggs, breadcrumbs, Parmesan, tomatoes, parsley, oregano, salt, and pepper. Mix well to combine.

2. Grease the inside of the slow cooker insert liberally with vegetable oil spray. Fold a sheet of heavy-duty aluminum foil in half, and place it in the bottom of the slow cooker with the sides of the foil extending up the sides of the slow cooker. Form meat mixture into an oval or round, depending on the shape of your cooker, and place it on top of the foil.

3. Cook meatloaf on Low for 6 to 8 hours or on High for 3 to 4 hours, or until an instant-read thermometer inserted into the center of meat registers 165°F.

4. Remove meatloaf from the slow cooker by pulling it up by the sides of the foil. Drain off any grease from the foil, slide meatloaf onto a serving platter, and serve hot with Herbed Tomato Sauce or marinara sauce.

Note: The dish can be prepared up to 2 days in advance and refrigerated, tightly covered. Reheat it, covered, in a 350°F oven for 20 to 25 minutes, or until hot.

Variations:

* Substitute a combination of ground pork and ground veal for the ground turkey. The cooking time remains the same.

* Place half the meat mixture in the slow cooker, and then add a row of halved hard-cooked eggs. Top with remaining meat mixture.

* Place half the meat mixture in the slow cooker, and then layer a mixture of 1 (10-ounce) package frozen chopped spinach, thawed and drained well, mixed with 1 large egg in the center. Top with the remaining meat mixture.

If you grow plum tomatoes in the summer you can make your own sun-dried tomatoes, or rather, oven-dried. Core, peel, and seed the tomatoes, and then place them on a wire cooling rack on top of a baking sheet. Sprinkle them with salt, pepper, and any fresh herb you like, and then bake them in a 150°F oven for 10 to 20 hours.

Duck Legs Braised in Red Wine

The slow cooker is a great way to cook duck; the meat becomes meltingly tender, and all the fat comes out from beneath the skin, which is browned before serving.

Makes 4 to 6 servings | *Prep time: 15 minutes* | *Minimum cook time: 7 hours in a medium slow cooker*

4 to 6 duck leg quarters

3 tablespoons olive oil

1 small onion, diced

3 garlic cloves, minced

1 carrot, chopped

1½ cups dry red wine

1 cup Chicken Stock (page 19) or purchased stock

⅓ cup chopped fresh parsley

1 tablespoon dried thyme or ½ teaspoon dried

1 bay leaf

2 teaspoons cornstarch

Salt and freshly ground black pepper to taste

1. Rinse duck and pat dry with paper towels. Using a metal skewer, prick the skin of each leg horizontally to the skin so that the skin but not the meat is pierced. Arrange duck legs in the slow cooker.

2. Heat oil in a medium skillet over medium-high heat. Add onion, garlic, and carrot, and cook, stirring frequently, for 3 minutes, or until onion is translucent. Add wine to the skillet, raise the heat to high, and boil wine until reduced by one-third. Pour mixture into the slow cooker.

3. Add stock, parsley, thyme, and bay leaf to the slow cooker, and stir well. Cook on Low for 7 to 9 hours, or until duck is incredibly tender. Remove and discard bay leaf.

4. Preheat the oven broiler, and line a broiler pan with heavy-duty aluminum foil. Remove duck from the slow cooker with a slotted spatula, and set aside. Pour braising liquid into a saucepan, and allow to sit undisturbed for 10 minutes. Spoon fat off of surface of sauce with a soup ladle.

5. Bring sauce to a boil over high heat, and reduce by half. Mix cornstarch with 2 tablespoons cold water, and mix into sauce. Cook for 2 minutes, or until juices are bubbly and slightly thickened. Season to taste with salt and pepper.

6. To serve, broil duck legs for 2 to 3 minutes, or until skin is crisp. Serve hot, passing sauce separately.

Note: The dish can be prepared up to 2 days in advance and refrigerated, tightly covered. Reheat it, covered, in a 350°F oven for 20 to 25 minutes, or until hot. Do not broil the duck legs until just prior to serving.

Variations:

* Add ½ cup pitted olives to the slow cooker.
* Add 1 pound baby carrots or ½ pound baby carrots and ½ pound parsnips, cut into 2-inch pieces to the slow cooker.

To *reduce* is to make something smaller, and when the word is used in cooking, it means to cut down on the volume of liquid by applying heat, which speeds evaporation. Simmering a gravy or sauce evaporates some of the water, which concentrates the flavor of the resulting liquid. Many recipes call for liquid to be reduced by half, but it can be a greater or smaller amount.

Chapter 7

Meat

Secondi

There are two reasons why this is the longest chapter in the book. The first reason is that cooking meats to exquisite tenderness is what the slow cooker does exceptionally well. And the second reason is that meat dishes are an essential part of Italian cuisine, especially when accompanied by an excellent Italian red wine.

Italy has the highest per capita consumption of veal, so there are ways to transform this delicate animal into stews, as well as many ways to cook cross-cut sections of its shank bones, called osso buco. Those recipes are followed by those for beef, lamb, and pork.

Often you can change the meat without sacrificing the quality of a recipe as long as the change is in the same flavor and texture family. For example, beef and lamb are interchangeable in recipes because both are hearty meats. In the same way, pork and veal are similar, and both can be substituted for whole pieces of chicken without changing the timing. The question you should ask yourself is: Is it a red meat or a white meat? Even though veal is a young cow, the flavor and texture is more similar to pork or chicken than it is to beef.

Even if you know nothing about beef and what the various parts are called, you can pick the right ones. Just look at the price tags. There are many more cuts on a cow that require long, slow cooking than there are parts that are meant to be grilled, broiled, or roasted. Look at the cost of a tenderloin roast, then look at the cost of a boneless chuck roast. Buy the chuck roast for the slow cooker.

Veal Marsala

Cooking veal in heady Marsala wine is a classic Italian preparation, and in this recipe the stew also contains lots of garlic, balanced by fresh parsley. Steamed or boiled potatoes make an excellent accompaniment.

Makes 4 to 6 servings | Prep time: 15 minutes | Minimum cook time: 3 hours in a medium slow cooker

2 pounds veal stew meat, fat trimmed, and cut into 1-inch cubes

All-purpose flour for dredging

¼ cup olive oil

6 garlic cloves, minced

½ cup chopped fresh parsley

¾ cup dry Marsala wine

¼ cup Chicken Stock (page 19) or purchased stock

Salt and freshly ground black pepper to taste

1. Coat veal with flour, shaking off any excess. Heat oil in a large skillet over medium-high heat. Add veal cubes, and brown on all sides. Remove veal from the pan with a slotted spoon, and transfer it to the slow cooker. Add garlic to the skillet. Cook, stirring constantly, for 1 minute. Scrape garlic into the slow cooker.

2. Add parsley, wine, and stock to the skillet, and bring to a boil, stirring to dislodge the brown bits in the skillet. Pour mixture into the slow cooker. Cook on Low for 6 to 8 hours or on High for 3 to 4 hours, or until veal is tender. Season to taste with salt and pepper to taste, and serve hot.

Note: The dish can be prepared up to 2 days in advance and refrigerated, tightly covered. Reheat it, covered, in a 350°F oven for 20 to 25 minutes, or until hot.

Variation:
* Substitute boneless pork shoulder or country ribs for the veal.

> While veal is a baby cow, it's so delicate that it's most often cooked with chicken stock rather than veal stock. The same is true for pork; beef stock is too assertive for the lighter meats.

Veal Stew with Acorn Squash

This stew is adapted from a wonderful recipe I tried from Joyce Goldstein's book *Cucina Ebraica: Flavors of the Italian Jewish Kitchen*. Joyce is a wonderful chef, and her Square One restaurant was one of my favorite spots in San Francisco. The recipe includes Marsala, but it is far subtler than Veal Marsala.

Makes 4 to 6 servings | Prep time: 15 minutes | Minimum cook time: 3 hours in a medium slow cooker

2 pounds veal stew meat, fat trimmed, and cut into 1-inch cubes

All-purpose flour for dredging

¼ cup olive oil

1 medium onion, diced

2 garlic cloves, minced

1 cup sweet Marsala wine

½ cup Chicken Stock (page 19) or purchased stock

1 (1-pound) acorn squash, peeled, seeded, and cut into ¾-inch cubes

2 tablespoons chopped fresh parsley

2 teaspoons fresh thyme or ¼ teaspoon dried

Salt and freshly ground black pepper to taste

1. Coat veal with flour, shaking off any excess. Heat oil in a large skillet over medium-high heat. Add veal cubes, and brown on all sides. Remove veal from the pan with a slotted spoon, and transfer it to the slow cooker. Add onion and garlic to the skillet. Cook, stirring frequently, for 3 minutes, or until onion is translucent. Scrape mixture into the slow cooker.

2. Add wine and stock to the skillet, and bring to a boil, stirring to dislodge the brown bits in the skillet. Pour mixture into the slow cooker. Add squash, parsley, and thyme to the slow cooker, and stir well.

3. Cook on Low for 6 to 8 hours or on High for 3 to 4 hours, or until veal is tender. Season to taste with salt and pepper, and serve hot.

Note: The dish can be prepared up to 2 days in advance and refrigerated, tightly covered. Reheat it, covered, in a 350°F oven for 20 to 25 minutes, or until hot.

Variation:

＊ Substitute butternut squash for the acorn squash.

Along with tomatoes and potatoes, squash is a recent addition to European cuisines and came from the New World. Squash seeds have been found in ancient Mexican archeological digs dating back to somewhere between 9000 and 4000 BCE. The first European settlers originally thought squash to be a type of melon since they had never seen them before.

Veal Stew with Bell Peppers

In this stew the veal is braised in red wine and flavored with a combination of fresh herbs. While in Italy red bell peppers are used, I like to use a combination of colors to make the dish even prettier.

Makes 4 to 6 servings | Prep time: 15 minutes | Minimum cook time: 3 hours in a medium slow cooker

2 pounds veal stew meat, fat trimmed, and cut into 1-inch cubes

All-purpose flour for dredging

¼ cup olive oil

2 garlic cloves, minced

¾ cup dry red wine

1 (14.5-ounce) can petite diced tomatoes, undrained

2 tablespoons chopped fresh parsley

2 tablespoons chopped fresh sage or 2 teaspoons dried

2 red bell peppers, seeds and ribs removed, and thinly sliced

Salt and freshly ground black pepper to taste

1. Coat veal with flour, shaking off any excess. Heat oil in a large skillet over medium-high heat. Add veal cubes, and brown on all sides. Remove veal from the pan with a slotted spoon, and transfer it to the slow cooker. Add garlic to the skillet. Cook, stirring constantly, for 1 minute. Scrape garlic into the slow cooker.

2. Add wine and tomatoes to the skillet, and bring to a boil, stirring to dislodge the brown bits in the skillet. Pour mixture into the slow cooker.

3. Add parsley and sage to the slow cooker, and stir well. Cook on Low for 5 to 7 hours or on High for 2½ to 3, or until veal is almost tender. If cooking on Low, raise the heat to High. Add peppers, and cook for 1 to 2 hours, or until veal is tender. Season to taste with salt and pepper to taste, and serve hot.

Note: The dish can be prepared up to 2 days in advance and refrigerated, tightly covered. Reheat it, covered, in a 350°F oven for 20 to 25 minutes, or until hot.

Variation:

✱ Substitute boneless, skinless chicken breasts or thighs for the veal. Reduce the total cooking time to 5 hours on Low or 2½ hours on High.

While it is not used as often now in Italian cooking as oregano or basil, sage dates back to Roman times. It was considered to have healing properties, particularly helpful in the digestion of the fatty meats of the time, and was deemed a part of the official Roman pharmocopeia.

Osso Buco with Mushrooms and Potatoes

This is a hearty veal shank recipe that is perfect for a crisp fall or winter evening. The combination of dried and fresh mushrooms meld with the red wine and herbs magically, and because the dish contains potatoes the meal is complete.

Makes 4 to 6 servings | Prep time: 25 minutes | Minimum cook time: 3 hours in a large slow cooker

1 ounce dried porcini mushrooms

1½ cups Beef Stock (page 21) or purchased stock

4 to 6 meaty veal shanks, about 2-inches thick

All-purpose flour for dredging

⅓ cup olive oil, divided

2 tablespoons unsalted butter

2 large onions, diced

3 garlic cloves, minced

1 pound cremini mushrooms, wiped with a damp paper towel, stemmed, and sliced

1 cup dry red wine

3 large redskin potatoes, scrubbed and cut into ¾-inch cubes

2 tablespoons chopped fresh parsley

1 tablespoon chopped fresh rosemary or 1 teaspoon dried

1 bay leaf

Salt and freshly ground black pepper to taste

1. Combine porcini mushrooms and stock in a saucepan, and bring to a boil over high heat, stirring occasionally. Soak mushrooms for 10 minutes, pressing mushrooms down with the back of a spoon to keep them submerged. Drain mushrooms, reserving soaking liquid, and chop mushrooms. Strain soaking liquid through a sieve lined with a paper coffee filter or a paper towel. Set aside.

2. Coat veal with flour, shaking off any excess. Heat ¼ cup oil in a large skillet over medium-high heat. Add as many veal shanks as will fit in a single layer, and brown them for 3 to 4 minutes per side, or until lightly browned. Work in batches if necessary. Transfer shanks into the slow cooker.

3. Add remaining olive oil and butter to the skillet. Add onions, garlic, and mushrooms. Cook, stirring frequently, 3 to 5 minutes, or until mushrooms soften. Scrape mixture into the slow cooker. Add wine, potatoes, parsley, rosemary, bay leaf, porcini, and soaking liquid to the slow cooker, and stir well.

4. Cook on Low for 7 to 8 hours or on High for 3 to 4 hours, or until meat is very tender. Remove as much fat as possible from the surface of the slow cooker with a soup ladle. Remove and discard bay leaf, season to taste with salt and pepper, and serve hot.

Note: The dish can be prepared up to 2 days in advance and refrigerated, tightly covered. Reheat it, covered, in a 350ºF oven for 20 to 25 minutes, or until hot.

Variation:

* Substitute 2-inch cubes of boneless pork shoulder or country ribs for the veal.

Osso buco has become synonymous with "veal shank" in this country as well as in Italy. Unlike lamb shanks, which are almost always braised whole, veal shanks are cut into crosswise slices. Osso buco means "pierced bone," and the marrow from the bone is considered such a delicacy that special marrow spoons are served with the dish.

Osso Buco alla Milanese

This is the classic preparation of veal shanks. They are braised in white wine and vegetables and topped with a sprinkling of garlic, lemon zest, and fresh herbs. Serve them with some rice.

Makes 4 to 6 servings | Prep time: 25 minutes | Minimum cook time: 3 hours in a large slow cooker

4 to 6 meaty veal shanks, about 2-inches thick

All-purpose flour for dredging

½ cup olive oil, divided

4 tablespoons unsalted butter

2 large onions, diced

3 garlic cloves, minced

2 carrots, diced

2 celery ribs, diced

½ cup dry white wine

1 (14.5-ounce) can crushed tomatoes in tomato puree

1 cup Chicken Stock (page 19) or purchased stock

2 tablespoons chopped fresh parsley

1 tablespoon fresh thyme or ½ teaspoon dried

1 bay leaf

1 (3-inch) slice lemon zest

Salt and freshly ground black pepper to taste

GREMOLATA

5 tablespoons chopped fresh parsley

6 garlic cloves, minced

2 tablespoons grated lemon zest

1 tablespoon grated orange zest

1. Rub veal shanks with flour, shaking off any extra over the sink or a plate. Heat ¼ cup oil in a large skillet over medium-high heat. Add as many veal shanks as will fit in a single layer, and brown them for 3 to 4 minutes per side, or until lightly browned. Work in batches if necessary. Transfer shanks into the slow cooker.

2. Add remaining ¼ cup olive oil and butter to the skillet. Add onions, garlic, carrots, and celery. Cook, stirring frequently, 3 minutes or until onions are translucent. Scrape mixture into the slow cooker. Stir in wine, tomatoes, stock, parsley, thyme, and bay leaf.

3. Cook on Low for 7 to 8 hours or on High for 3 to 4 hours, or until meat is very tender. Remove as much fat as possible from the surface of the slow cooker with a soup ladle. Remove and discard bay leaf and lemon zest, and season to taste with salt and pepper.

4. While shanks are cooking, prepare Gremolata. Combine parsley, garlic, lemon zest, and orange zest in a small mixing bowl. Serve veal shanks hot with a sprinkling of topping.

Note: The dish can be prepared up to 2 days in advance and refrigerated, tightly covered. Reheat it, covered, in a 350°F oven for 20 to 25 minutes, or until hot.

Variation:

✳ Add ¾ cup pitted kalamata olives to the slow cooker. If using olives, chances are no additional salt will be needed.

When you're browning meat coated with flour, browning the flour is even more important than browning the meat. This step creates a sauce that thickens slightly but does not taste pasty. If you don't want to brown the veal, thicken the juices with cornstarch instead.

Osso Buco with Garbanzo Beans

Garbanzo beans add their nutty flavor and soft texture to this version of veal shanks, served with gremolata.

Makes 4 to 6 servings | Prep time: 25 minutes | Minimum cook time: 3 hours in a large slow cooker

4 to 6 meaty veal shanks, about 2-inches thick

All-purpose flour for dredging

½ cup olive oil, divided

1 large onions, diced

2 garlic cloves, minced

2 carrots, diced

2 celery ribs, diced

1 (28-ounce) can diced tomatoes, drained

1 cup dry white wine

2 tablespoons chopped fresh parsley

1 tablespoon fresh thyme or ½ teaspoon dried

2 bay leaves

1 (3-inch) strip lemon zest

1 (15-ounce) can garbanzo beans, drained and rinsed

Salt and freshly ground black pepper to taste

GREMOLATA

5 tablespoons chopped fresh parsley

6 garlic cloves, minced

2 tablespoons grated lemon zest

1 tablespoon grated orange zest

1. Coat veal with flour, shaking off any excess. Heat ¼ cup oil in a large skillet over medium-high heat. Add as many veal shanks as will fit in a single layer, and brown them for 3 to 4 minutes per side, or until lightly browned. Work in batches if necessary. Transfer shanks into the slow cooker.

2. Add remaining oil to the skillet. Add onions, garlic, carrots, and celery. Cook, stirring frequently, 3 minutes, or until onions are translucent. Scrape mixture into the slow cooker. Add tomatoes, wine, parsley, thyme, bay leaves, and lemon zest to the slow cooker, and stir well.

3. Cook on Low for 6 to 8 hours or on High for 3 to 4 hours, or until meat is very tender. If cooking on Low, raise the heat to High. Add beans, and cook for 10 to 20 minutes, or until stew is bubbly again. Remove as much fat as possible from the surface of the slow cooker with a soup ladle. Remove and discard bay leaves and lemon zest, and season to taste with salt and pepper.

4. While shanks are cooking, prepare Gremolata. Combine parsley, garlic, lemon zest, and orange zest in a small mixing bowl. Serve veal shanks hot with a sprinkling of topping.

Note: The dish can be prepared up to 2 days in advance and refrigerated, tightly covered. Reheat it, covered, in a 350°F oven for 20 to 25 minutes, or until hot.

Variation:

✳ Substitute cannellini beans for the garbanzo beans.

Zest really does have something to do with *zesty*; it's the thin, colored outer portion of the citrus skin that contains all the aromatic oils. The white pith just beneath it is bitter, so you should take pains to separate the zest from the fruit without also taking any pith with it. Remove the zest using a special citrus zester, a vegetable peeler, or a paring knife. You can also grate it off using the fine holes of a box grater.

Marinated Pot Roast in Mustard Sauce

This version of pot roast comes from the Piedmont, which is also home to justly famous Barolo wine, and there's a bit of mustard in the sauce that stands up to the character of that wine. Serve it with some oven-roasted potatoes.

Makes 4 to 6 servings | Prep time: 20 minutes | Minimum cook time: 5 hours in a medium slow cooker

1 (2- to 2½-pound) beef rump or chuck roast

1 (750 ml) bottle dry red wine

1 medium onion, chopped

1 celery rib, chopped

3 garlic cloves, minced

2 tablespoons fresh thyme or 1 teaspoon dried

1 bay leaf

Salt and freshly ground black pepper to taste

2 teaspoons cornstarch

3 tablespoons Dijon mustard, or to taste

1. Rinse meat, and trim of visible fat. Combine wine, onion, celery, garlic, thyme, bay leaf, salt, and pepper in a heavy resealable plastic bag, and mix well. Add beef, and push out as much air as possible from the bag before closing. Marinate beef, refrigerated, for at least 12 hours, and up to 2 days, turning the bag occasionally.

2. Preheat the oven broiler, and line a broiler pan with heavy-duty aluminum foil. Remove meat from marinade, reserving marinade, and pat beef dry with paper towels. Broil beef for 3 minutes per side or until browned. Transfer beef to the slow cooker, and pour in any juices that have collected in the pan.

3. Pour marinade into the slow cooker. Cook on Low for 10 to 12 hours or on High for 5 to 6 hours, or until beef is very tender.

4. If cooking on Low, raise the heat to High. Mix cornstarch with 2 tablespoons cold water, and stir cornstarch mixture and mustard into the slow cooker. Cook for an additional 15 to 20 minutes, or until juices are bubbling and slightly thickened. Remove and discard bay leaf, season to taste with salt and pepper, and serve hot.

Note: The dish can be prepared up to 2 days in advance and refrigerated, tightly covered. Reheat it, covered, in a 350ºF oven for 20 to 25 minutes, or until hot.

Variation:
* Substitute 2 tablespoons tomato paste for the mustard.

> **Marinating serves two purposes, and it is especially useful for inexpensive cuts of meat. The acid in wine breaks down the meat fibers to tenderize the cut as well as giving it color and flavor.**

Short Ribs of Beef with Rosemary and Fennel

Short ribs of beef are one of my favorite cuts because they become so meltingly tender when slowly braised in the slow cooker. The aromatic rosemary in the simple sauce cuts through the richness of the meat well.

Makes 4 to 6 servings | Prep time: 15 minutes | Minimum cook time: 4 hours in a large slow cooker

5 pounds meaty short ribs with bones, or 2 pounds boneless short ribs

¼ cup olive oil

1 large onion, diced

4 garlic cloves, minced

2 cups Beef Stock (page 21) or purchased stock

1 large fennel bulb, cored, trimmed, and sliced

2 tablespoons chopped fresh parsley

3 tablespoons chopped fresh rosemary or 1 tablespoon dried

2 teaspoons cornstarch

Salt and freshly ground black pepper to taste

1. Preheat the oven broiler, and line a broiler pan with heavy-duty aluminum foil. Broil short ribs for 3 to 4 minutes per side, or until browned. Arrange short ribs in the slow cooker, and pour in any juices that have collected in the pan.

2. Heat oil in a medium skillet over medium-high heat. Add onion and garlic, and cook, stirring frequently, for 3 minutes, or until onion is translucent. Scrape mixture into the slow cooker. Add stock, fennel, parsley, and rosemary to the slow cooker, and stir well.

3. Cook on Low for 8 to 10 hours or on High for 4 to 5 hours, or until short ribs are very tender. Remove as much grease as possible from the slow cooker with a soup ladle.

4. If cooking on Low, raise the heat to High. Mix cornstarch with 2 tablespoons cold water in a small cup. Stir cornstarch mixture into the cooker, and cook on High for 15 to 20 minutes, or until juices are bubbling and slightly thickened. Season to taste with salt and pepper, and serve hot.

Note: The dish can be prepared up to 2 days in advance and refrigerated, tightly covered. Reheat it, covered, in a 350°F oven for 20 to 25 minutes, or until hot.

Variation:
* Substitute 2½ pounds pork loin for the beef, and substitute chicken stock for the beef stock.

Our English word beef comes from the Latin *bos*, which means "ox." By the Middle Ages, it had become *boef* or beef in English. There were cattle at the Jamestown settlement in Virginia in the early seventeenth century, but the Texas longhorns that we use for beef today were brought to that state by the Spanish almost a century after the Jamestown settlement.

Chianti Beef Stew

All of the great European wine-producing regions—from Chianti to Burgundy and Rioja—have a dish similar to this straightforward but delicious stew. The meat is simmered in lightly seasoned wine with some vegetables added. Serve it with steamed or roasted potatoes, and more red wine.

Makes 4 to 6 servings | Prep time: 25 minutes | Minimum cook time: 4 hours in a medium slow cooker

2 pounds stewing beef, fat trimmed and cut into 2-inch cubes

2 tablespoons olive oil

1 large onion, diced

3 garlic cloves, minced

½ pound white mushrooms, wiped with a damp paper towel, stemmed, and sliced

2 carrots, thinly sliced

2 cups Chianti or other dry red wine

½ cup Beef Stock (page 21) or purchased stock

1 (14.5-ounce) can diced tomatoes, undrained

1 tablespoon tomato paste

2 tablespoons chopped fresh parsley

1 bay leaf

1 tablespoon cornstarch

1 cup fresh peas or frozen peas, thawed (optional)

Salt and freshly ground black pepper to taste

1. Preheat the oven broiler, and line a broiler pan with heavy-duty aluminum foil. Broil beef for 3 minutes per side or until browned. Transfer beef to the slow cooker, and pour in any juices that have collected in the pan.

2. Heat olive oil in a medium skillet over medium-high heat. Add onion, garlic, and mushrooms. Cook, stirring frequently, for 4 to 5 minutes, or until onion is translucent and mushrooms are soft. Scrape mixture into the slow cooker.

3. Add carrots, wine, stock, tomatoes, tomato paste, parsley, and bay leaf to the slow cooker, and stir well. Cook on Low for 8 to 10 hours or on High for 4 to 5 hours, or until beef is tender.

4. If cooking on Low, raise the heat to High. Mix cornstarch and 2 tablespoons cold water in a small cup, and stir cornstarch mixture and peas, if using, into beef. Cook for an additional 15 to 20 minutes, or until juices are bubbling and slightly thickened. Remove and discard bay leaf, season to taste with salt and pepper, and serve hot.

Note: The dish can be prepared up to 2 days in advance and refrigerated, tightly covered. Reheat it, covered, in a 350°F oven for 20 to 25 minutes, or until hot.

Variation:

* Substitute boneless lamb shoulder for the beef, and add 2 tablespoons chopped fresh rosemary to the slow cooker.

While I am adamant about fresh food, one exception to that rule is garden peas. Like the fate of fresh corn, the sugars begin to convert to starch almost immediately. That's why for both vegetables, if you can't find really fresh versions it's better to use frozen, which are processed when very fresh and remain sweet.

Beef Stew with Paprika

While we think of Italian regions as being Mediterranean, Trieste is very near the border with Austria and Hungary, so this stew from that region is made with Hungary's prime seasoning, paprika. To keep the metaphor going, serve it with some buttered egg noodles.

Makes 4 to 6 servings | Prep time: 25 minutes | Minimum cook time: 4 hours in a medium slow cooker

2 pounds stewing beef, fat trimmed and cut into 2-inch cubes

All-purpose flour for dredging

3 tablespoons olive oil

1 large onion, diced

3 garlic cloves, minced

2 tablespoons sweet paprika

2 teaspoons ground cumin

1 cup dry red wine

1 cup Beef Stock (page 21) or purchased stock

1 (14.5-ounce) can diced tomatoes, undrained

2 tablespoons chopped fresh parsley

2 tablespoons chopped fresh rosemary or 2 teaspoons dried

1 bay leaf

Salt and freshly ground black pepper to taste

1. Coat beef with flour, shaking off any excess. Heat oil in a large skillet over medium-high heat. Add beef cubes, and brown on all sides. Remove beef from the pan with a slotted spoon, and transfer it to the slow cooker. Add onion and garlic to the skillet. Cook, stirring frequently, for 3 minutes, or until onion is translucent. Add paprika and cumin, and cook for 1 minute, stirring constantly. Scrape mixture into the slow cooker.

2. Add wine to the skillet, and bring to a boil, stirring to dislodge the brown bits in the skillet. Pour mixture into the slow cooker.

3. Add stock, tomatoes, parsley, rosemary, and bay leaf to the slow cooker, and stir well. Cook on Low for 8 to 10 hours or on High for 4 to 5 hours, or until beef is tender. Remove and discard bay leaf, season to taste with salt and pepper, and serve hot.

Note: The dish can be prepared up to 2 days in advance and refrigerated, tightly covered. Reheat it, covered, in a 350°F oven for 20 to 25 minutes, or until hot.

Variation:

* Substitute boneless lamb shoulder for the beef, and add 2 tablespoons chopped fresh rosemary to the slow cooker.

An easy way to coat food with flour is to place the flour and food in a heavy plastic bag. Keep the air in the bag so the food can move around freely, and hold the top tightly closed with your hand. Shake the food around, and it will be evenly coated.

Stuffed Peppers

Herbs, salty prosciutto, and cooked rice are joined with beef to stuff these peppers, which are really a meal in themselves with a loaf of crusty bread.

Makes 4 to 6 servings | Prep time: 25 minutes | Minimum cook time: 2¹/₂ hours in a large slow cooker

4 to 6 large bell peppers

2 tablespoons olive oil

1 medium onion, diced

2 garlic cloves, minced

1 pound lean ground beef

2 tablespoons chopped fresh parsley

1 tablespoon chopped fresh oregano or 1 teaspoon dried

¾ cup cooked rice

½ cup chopped prosciutto or ham

½ cup freshly grated Parmesan cheese

1 large egg, lightly beaten

Salt and freshly ground black pepper to taste

1 cup Herbed Tomato Sauce (page 97) or purchased sauce

1. Cut top 1 inch off peppers. Remove and discard seeds from bottom of peppers. Discard stems from peppers, and chop flesh from tops.

2. Heat oil in a medium skillet over medium-high heat. Add onion, garlic, and chopped peppers. Cook, stirring frequently, for 3 minutes, or until onion is translucent. Scrape mixture into a mixing bowl. Crumble beef into the skillet, and cook for 3 minutes, breaking up lumps with a fork, or until browned. Transfer beef to the mixing bowl with a slotted spoon.

3. Add parsley, oregano, rice, prosciutto, Parmesan, eggs, salt, and pepper to the mixing bowl, and mix well. Divide the mixture into peppers, stuffing them loosely, and arrange peppers in the slow cooker. Pour tomato sauce over peppers.

4. Cook on Low for 5 to 7 hours or on High for 2¹/₂ to 3 hours, or until peppers are tender. Serve hot, spooning sauce on top of peppers.

Note: The dish can be prepared up to 2 days in advance and refrigerated, tightly covered. Reheat it, covered, in a 350°F oven for 20 to 25 minutes, or until hot.

Variations:

✳ Substitute ground turkey for the ground beef.

✳ Substitute cooked orzo or riso for the rice.

You can prolong the life of fresh herbs longer if you treat them like a bunch of flowers. Trim the stems when you bring them in from the market, and stick the stems into a glass of cold water. Keep them refrigerated.

Beef and Sausage Meatloaf

Polpette is the Italian word for meatball, and a huge meatball, or what we call a meatloaf, is called a *polpettone* (pronounced *pohl-peh-TOH-neh*). This dish combines ground beef with flavorful sausage, with lots of vegetables added too.

Makes 4 to 6 servings | *Prep time: 20 minutes* | *Minimum cook time: 3 hours in a medium slow cooker*

2 tablespoons olive oil

1 medium onion, chopped

1 small carrot, chopped

1 celery rib, chopped

1 garlic clove, minced

2 large eggs, lightly beaten

¼ cup whole milk

½ cup Italian breadcrumbs

½ cup freshly grated Parmesan cheese

½ cup grated mozzarella cheese

3 tablespoons chopped fresh parsley

1 tablespoon fresh thyme or ½ teaspoon dried

Salt and freshly ground black pepper to taste

1 pound lean ground beef

½ pound bulk sweet Italian sausage

1 cup Herbed Tomato Sauce (page 97) or purchased sauce

¼ cup dry red wine

Vegetable oil spray

1. Heat oil in a small skillet over medium-high heat. Add onion, carrot, celery, and garlic, and cook, stirring frequently, for 3 minutes, or until onion is translucent. Set aside.

2. Combine eggs, milk, breadcrumbs, Parmesan, mozzarella, parsley, thyme, salt, and pepper in a large mixing bowl, and stir well. Add beef, sausage, and vegetable mixture, and mix well.

3. Grease the inside of the slow cooker insert liberally with vegetable oil spray. Fold a sheet of heavy-duty aluminum foil in half, and place it in the bottom of the slow cooker with the sides of the foil extending up the sides of the slow cooker. Form meat mixture into an oval or round, depending on the shape of your cooker, and place it into the cooker on top of the foil. Combine tomato sauce and wine, and pour mixture on top of meatloaf.

4. Cook meatloaf on Low for 6 to 8 hours or on High for 3 to 4 hours, or until an instant-read thermometer inserted into the center of the loaf registers 165°F. Allow meatloaf to sit for 10 minutes. Remove meatloaf from the slow cooker by pulling it up by the sides of the foil. Drain off any grease from the foil, and slide meatloaf onto a serving platter. Serve immediately.

Note: The dish can be prepared up to 2 days in advance and refrigerated, tightly covered. Reheat it, covered, in a 350°F oven for 20 to 25 minutes, or until hot.

Variations:

✳ Substitute ground turkey for the beef and sausage; the cooking time will remain the same.

✳ Place a row of hard-cooked eggs in the center of the meatloaf before cooking.

✳ Add ½ pound diced sautéed mushrooms.

✳ Add 1 cup frozen chopped spinach, thawed and squeezed dry.

Italian breadcrumbs are toasted breadcrumbs that are then seasoned with parsley, other herbs, garlic, and Parmesan cheese. If you only have plain breadcrumbs, to replicate the flavor, add 1 teaspoon Italian seasoning, ½ teaspoon garlic powder, and 3 tablespoons Parmesan cheese to each 1 cup plain breadcrumbs.

Beef and Eggplant Stew

This is a great fall dish, when eggplants and bell peppers are still growing in the garden but the evenings are cool enough to want some comfort food. The combination of balsamic vinegar and brown sugar give the dish a very slight sweet and sour note.

Makes 4 to 6 servings | Active time: 25 minutes | Minimum cook time: 5 hours in a medium slow cooker

1 (1-pound) eggplant, trimmed and cut into ¾-inch dice

Salt

1 (2-pound) chuck roast, trimmed and cut into 1-inch cubes (or 1½ pounds stewing beef)

⅓ cup olive oil, divided

1 medium onion, chopped

3 garlic cloves, minced

1 green bell pepper, seeds and ribs removed, and thinly sliced

1¼ cups dry red wine

2 tablespoons balsamic vinegar

2 tablespoons firmly packed light brown sugar

1 (8-ounce) can tomato sauce

3 tablespoons chopped fresh parsley

1 tablespoon fresh chopped marjoram or 1 teaspoon dried

2 bay leaves

2 teaspoons cornstarch

Freshly ground black pepper to taste

1. Place eggplant in a colander, and sprinkle cubes liberally with salt. Place a plate on top of eggplant cubes, and weight the plate with some cans. Place the colander in the sink or on a plate, and allow eggplant to drain for 30 minutes. Rinse eggplant cubes, and squeeze hard to remove water.

Wring out remaining water with a cloth tea towel.

2. While eggplant sits, preheat the oven broiler, and line a broiler pan with heavy-duty aluminum foil. Broil beef for 3 minutes per side, or until browned. Transfer beef to the slow cooker, and pour in any juices that have collected in the pan.

3. Heat ½ of olive oil in a medium skillet over medium heat. Add onion, garlic, and green pepper. Cook, stirring frequently, for 3 minutes, or until onion is translucent. Scrape mixture into the slow cooker.

4. Heat remaining olive oil in a large skillet over medium-high heat. Add eggplant cubes, and cook, stirring frequently, for 3 minutes, or until eggplant begins to soften. Transfer eggplant to the slow cooker.

5. Add wine, vinegar, brown sugar, tomato sauce, parsley, marjoram, and bay leaves to the slow cooker, and stir well. Cook on Low for 8 to 10 hours or on High for 4 to 5 hours, or until beef and vegetables are tender.

6. If cooking on Low, raise the heat to High. Mix cornstarch and 2 tablespoons cold water in a small cup, and stir cornstarch mixture into beef. Cook for an additional 10 to 20 minutes, or until juices are bubbling and slightly thickened. Remove and discard bay leaves, season to taste with salt and pepper, and serve hot.

Note: The dish can be prepared up to 2 days in advance and refrigerated, tightly covered. Reheat it, covered, in a 350°F oven for 20 to 25 minutes, or until hot.

Variation:
* Substitute lamb shanks or cubes of boneless lamb shoulder for the beef. Add 1 tablespoon chopped fresh rosemary to the slow cooker.

> If you don't have any balsamic vinegar, cider vinegar with a bit of sugar or molasses is the best substitute.

Lamb Shanks with Olives and Artichoke Hearts

While "white meats" are frequently cooked in red wine, it's unusual for red meats to be cooked in white wine. But that's the basis of this dish, punctuated by salty black olives and delicate artichoke hearts.

Makes 4 to 6 servings | Active time: 20 minutes | Minimum cook time: 4 hours in a large slow cooker

4 to 6 (12- to 14-ounce) lamb shanks

3 tablespoons olive oil

1 large sweet onion, diced

3 garlic cloves, minced

1 cup Beef Stock (page 21) or purchased stock

1 (8-ounce) can tomato sauce

1 cup dry white wine

2 tablespoons chopped fresh rosemary or 1 tablespoon dried

2 tablespoons chopped fresh parsley

12 baby artichokes, trimmed with outer leaves removed, and halved

½ cup pitted black oil-cured olives

1 tablespoon cornstarch

Salt and freshly ground black pepper to taste

1. Preheat the oven broiler, and line a broiler pan with heavy-duty aluminum foil. Broil lamb shanks for 3 minutes per side, or until browned. Transfer lamb to the slow cooker, and pour in any juices that have collected in the pan.

2. Heat oil in a medium skillet over medium-high heat. Add onion and garlic, and cook, stirring frequently, for 3 minutes, or until onion is translucent. Scrape mixture into the slow cooker. Add stock, tomato sauce, wine, rosemary, and parsley to the slow cooker, and stir well.

3. Cook shanks on Low for 6 to 8 hours or on High for 3 to 4 hours, or until lamb is almost tender. Add artichokes and olives to the slow cooker, and cook for 2 hours on Low or 1 hour on High.

4. If cooking on Low, raise the heat to High. Mix cornstarch with 2 tablespoons cold water in a small cup. Add cornstarch mixture to the slow cooker, cover, and cook for an additional 10 to 15 minutes, or until the juices are bubbling and slightly thickened. Season to taste with salt and pepper, and serve hot.

Note: The dish can be prepared up to 2 days in advance and refrigerated, tightly covered. Reheat it, covered, in a 350°F oven for 20 to 25 minutes, or until hot.

Variation:

❋ Substitute short ribs of beef on the bone for the lamb shanks. The cooking time will remain the same.

Like apples and avocados, artichokes darken when exposed to air. When preparing them have a bowl of cold water acidulated with lemon juice on the counter. Drop the artichokes into it as you trim the stems and pull of the outer leaves.

Lamb Stew with Onions and Potatoes

Cipollini onions look like tiny hockey pucks when you see them in the market, and they hold their shape very well when braised. This stew is a one-dish meal, since it also contains potatoes.

Makes 4 to 6 servings | Prep time: 25 minutes | Minimum cook time: 4 hours in a large slow cooker

1 pound cipollini onions

2 pounds boneless lamb shoulder or leg of lamb, fat trimmed and cut into 2-inch cubes

All-purpose flour for dredging

¼ cup olive oil

1 small yellow onion, diced

3 garlic cloves, minced

1 cup dry red wine

12 small redskin potatoes, scrubbed and halved

2 carrots, thickly sliced

1½ cup Beef Stock (page 21) or purchased stock

1 (14.5-ounce) can diced tomatoes, undrained

2 tablespoons chopped fresh parsley

1 bay leaf

Salt and freshly ground black pepper to taste

1. Bring a saucepan of water to a boil. Add the cippolini onions, and boil for 1 minute. Drain onions, and run cold tap water over them. Peel onions, and trim off root end, keeping onions whole. Arrange onions in the slow cooker.

2. Coat lamb with flour, shaking off any excess. Heat oil in a large skillet over medium-high heat. Add lamb cubes, and brown on all sides. Remove lamb from the pan with a slotted spoon, and transfer it to the slow cooker. Add yellow onion and garlic to the skillet. Cook, stirring frequently, for 3 minutes, or until onion is translucent. Scrape mixture into the slow cooker.

3. Add wine to the skillet, and bring to a boil, stirring to dislodge the brown bits in the skillet. Pour mixture into the slow cooker. Add potatoes, carrots, stock, tomatoes, parsley, and bay leaf to the slow cooker, and stir well.

4. Cook on Low for 8 to 10 hours or on High for 4 to 5 hours, or until lamb and vegetables are tender. Remove and discard bay leaf, season to taste with salt and pepper to taste, and serve hot.

Note: The dish can be prepared up to 2 days in advance and refrigerated, tightly covered. Reheat it, covered, in a 350°F oven for 20 to 25 minutes, or until hot.

Variation:

* Substitute cubes of beef chuck for the lamb shoulder.

If you see a potato that has a greenish tinge, it means it was exposed to light. Cut away that portion of the potato because the green flesh can be toxic. Store potatoes in a cool, dry place—but not with onions. Onions give off a natural gas that can cause potatoes to rot more quickly.

Lamb Stew with Prosciutto and Bell Peppers

Lamb is an inherently rich meat, and the sweetness of red bell peppers combined with bits of salty prosciutto serve as perfect foils to that richness. Serve this stew with some crusty bread to enjoy the sauce.

Makes 4 to 6 servings | *Prep time: 20 minutes* | *Minimum cook time: 4 hours in a medium slow cooker*

2 pounds boneless lamb shoulder or leg of lamb, fat trimmed and cut into 2-inch cubes

All-purpose flour for dredging

¼ cup olive oil

1 medium onion, diced

3 garlic cloves, minced

¼ pound prosciutto, cut into ½-inch cubes

1 cup dry red wine

1 cup Beef Stock (page 21) or purchased stock

2 tablespoons chopped fresh rosemary or 2 teaspoons dried

2 tablespoons chopped fresh sage or 2 teaspoons dried

2 tablespoons chopped fresh parsley

1 large red bell pepper, seeds and ribs removed, and thinly sliced

Salt and freshly ground black pepper to taste

1. Coat lamb with flour, shaking off any excess. Heat oil in a large skillet over medium-high heat. Add lamb cubes, and brown on all sides. Remove lamb from the pan with a slotted spoon, and transfer it to the slow cooker. Add onion, garlic, and prosciutto to the skillet. Cook, stirring frequently, for 3 minutes, or until onion is translucent. Scrape mixture into the slow cooker.

2. Add wine to the skillet, and bring to a boil, stirring to dislodge the brown bits in the skillet. Pour mixture into the slow cooker. Add stock, rosemary, sage, and parsley to the slow cooker, and stir well.

3. Cook on Low for 7 to 9 hours or on High for 3½ to 4 hours, or until lamb is almost tender. If cooking on Low, raise the heat to High. Add peppers, and cook for 1 to 2 hours, or until lamb is tender. Season to taste with salt and pepper to taste, and serve hot.

Note: The dish can be prepared up to 2 days in advance and refrigerated, tightly covered. Reheat it, covered, in a 350°F oven for 20 to 25 minutes, or until hot.

Variation:

✳ Substitute cubes of beef chuck for the lamb shoulder.

An easy way to cut bell peppers is to start by slicing off the bottom so the pepper sits flat on the cutting board. Then hold the pepper by its stem and slice down along the rounded curves between the indentations. The indentations are the ribs, so you end up with the ribs and seeds like a skeleton, which you can then discard.

Lamb, Sausage, and Bean Stew

This stew is like an Italian version of the famed southwestern French dish, Cassoulet. Tender cubes of lamb and sausage are baked with beans in an herbed sauce. This is a wonderful party dish because it requires only a fork.

Makes 8 to 10 servings | Prep time: 25 minutes | Minimum cook time: 5½ hours in a large slow cooker

1 pound dried cannellini beans

¼ cup olive oil

1 large sweet onion, such as Vidalia or Bermuda, diced

5 garlic cloves, minced

2 cups Chicken Stock (page 19) or purchased stock

1 cup dry white wine

1 (14.5-oounce) can diced tomatoes, undrained

3 tablespoons tomato paste

3 tablespoons chopped fresh parsley

1 tablespoon fresh thyme or ½ teaspoon dried

1 bay leaf

1½ pounds boneless lamb shoulder or leg of lamb, fat trimmed and cut into 2-inch cubes

1 pound lugenega, or other fresh Italian sausage links, pricked with the tip of a paring knife

Salt and freshly ground black pepper to taste

1. Rinse beans in a colander and place them in a mixing bowl covered with cold water. Allow beans to soak for at least six hours, or overnight. Or place beans into a saucepan and bring to a boil over high heat. Boil 1 minute. Turn off the heat, cover the pan, and soak beans for 1 hour. With either soaking method, drain beans, discard soaking water, and begin cooking as soon as possible.

2. Heat oil in a medium skillet over medium-high heat. Add onions and garlic, and cook, stirring frequently, for 3 minutes or until onions are translucent. Scrape mixture into the slow cooker.

3. Add drained beans, stock, wine, tomatoes, tomato paste, parsley, thyme, and bay leaf to the slow cooker, and stir well. Cook bean mixture for 4 hours on Low or 2 hours on High.

4. Preheat the oven broiler, and line a broiler pan with heavy-duty aluminum foil. Broil lamb and sausages for 3 minutes per side, or until browned. Transfer meats to the slow cooker, and pour in any juices that have collected in the pan. Cook on Low for 8 to 10 hours or on High for 4 to 5 hours, or until lamb and beans are tender. Remove and discard bay leaf, season to taste with salt and pepper to taste, and serve hot.

Note: The dish can be prepared up to 2 days in advance and refrigerated, tightly covered. Reheat it, covered, in a 350°F oven for 20 to 25 minutes, or until hot.

Variation:
* Substitute beef chuck for the lamb shoulder, and substitute beef stock for the chicken stock.

Here's a tip from traditional Spanish cooking: Add a wine cork or two to a braised meat dish before cooking it, either conventionally or in the slow cooker. The cork releases enzymes that help the meat become tender.

Lamb Shanks Cacciatore

Woody wild mushrooms and aromatic orange zest create a complex flavor for these meaty lamb shanks braised in red wine. Serve them with some Farro Pilaf (page 235) or mashed potatoes.

Makes 4 to 6 servings | Active time: 20 minutes | Minimum cook time: 4 hours in a large slow cooker

4 to 6 (12- to 14-ounce) lamb shanks

3 tablespoons olive oil

1 large sweet onion, diced

1 teaspoon granulated sugar

Salt and freshly ground black pepper to taste

3 garlic cloves, minced

½ cup dried porcini mushrooms

2 cups Beef Stock (page 21) or purchased stock

2 juice oranges, washed

1½ cups dry red wine

3 tablespoons tomato paste

3 tablespoons chopped fresh rosemary or 1 tablespoon dried

2 tablespoons chopped fresh parsley

2 bay leaves

1 tablespoon cornstarch

1. Preheat the oven broiler, and line a broiler pan with heavy-duty aluminum foil. Broil lamb shanks for 3 minutes per side, or until browned. Transfer lamb to the slow cooker, and pour in any juices that have collected in the pan.

2. Heat oil in a skillet over medium heat. Add onions, sugar, salt, and pepper, and toss to coat onions. Cover the pan, and cook for 10 minutes, stirring occasionally. Uncover the pan, and cook over medium-high heat, stirring frequently, for 10 to 15 minutes, or until the onions are browned. Reduce the heat to low, stir in garlic, and cook for 1 minute, stirring constantly. Scrape mixture into the slow cooker.

3. While onions cook, combine mushrooms and stock in a small saucepan. Bring to a boil over high heat, remove the pan from the heat, and allow mushrooms to soak for 10 minutes. Remove mushrooms from stock with a slotted spoon, and chop. Strain stock through a sieve lined with a paper coffee filter or paper towel. Add mushrooms and stock to the slow cooker, and stir well.

4. Grate zest and squeeze juice from oranges. Add zest and orange juice to the slow cooker along with wine, tomato paste, rosemary, parsley, and bay leaves, and stir well. Cook shanks on Low for 8 to 10 hours or on High for 4 to 5 hours, or until lamb is very tender.

5. If cooking on Low, raise the heat to High. Mix cornstarch with 2 tablespoons cold water in a small cup. Add cornstarch mixture to the slow cooker, cover, and cook for an additional 10 to 15 minutes, or until the juices are bubbling and slightly thickened. Remove and discard bay leaves, season to taste with salt and pepper, and serve hot.

Note: The dish can be prepared up to 2 days in advance and refrigerated, tightly covered. Reheat it, covered, in a 350ºF oven for 20 to 25 minutes, or until hot.

Variations:

✳ Substitute short ribs of beef on the bone for the lamb shanks. The cooking time will remain the same.

✳ Rather than browning the shanks in the broiler, smoke them on a charcoal grill adding soaked mesquite chips to the coals.

Frequently, lamb shanks have a shiny membrane over the lower part of the bone. But unlike the shiny membrane on beef or pork tenderloin, it's not really necessary to trim this off. It will become tender after the long hours of cooking.

Herbed Pork Roast

It was in an outdoor market in Umbria that I first discovered this meltingly tender aromatic and flavorful pork called *porchetta* (pronounced *poor-KHET-ah*). The key to the success of this dish is using fresh herbs, and it's even better if you season it the night before you're cooking it.

Makes 6 to 8 servings | Prep time: 15 minutes | Minimum cook time: 6 hours in a medium slow cooker

1 (2-pound) boneless pork roast, preferably shoulder

6 garlic cloves, minced

¼ cup fresh chopped rosemary

2 tablespoons chopped fresh parsley

2 tablespoons chopped fresh sage

Salt and freshly ground black pepper to taste

3 celery ribs, cut into 4-inch lengths

⅓ cup Chicken Stock (page 19) or purchased stock

1. Rinse pork and pat dry with paper towels. Combine garlic, rosemary, parsley, sage, salt and pepper in a mixing bowl. Make slits deep into pork, and stuff half of mixture into the slits. Rub remaining mixture on the outside of pork. Arrange celery in the bottom of the slow cooker to form a trivet.

2. Preheat the oven broiler, and line a broiler pan with heavy-duty aluminum foil. Broil pork for 3 minutes per side, or until browned. Transfer pork to the slow cooker, and pour in any juices that have collected in the pan. Pour stock over pork.

3. Cook on High for 2 hours, then reduce the heat to Low and cook for 4 hours, or until pork is fork tender. Carve pork into slices, and moisten with pan juices from the slow cooker. Serve hot.

Note: The dish can be prepared up to 2 days in advance and refrigerated, tightly covered. Reheat it, covered, in a 350°F oven for 20 to 25 minutes, or until hot.

Variation:

✳ Substitute a boned and rolled breast of veal for the pork. The cooking time will remain the same.

> Browning meat under the broiler accomplishes two things when using a slow cooker. It gives the meat a more appealing color, and it heats it so that it passes through the "danger zone" of 40°F to 140°F faster, especially if you're cooking on Low.

Braised Pork Chops

A combination of Marsala and red wine forms the sauce for these chops, which are delicious served with oven-roasted potatoes.

Makes 4 to 6 servings | Prep time: 20 minutes | Minimum cook time: 3¹/₂ hours in a medium slow cooker

4 to 6 (6-ounce) boneless pork loin chops

2 tablespoons olive oil

2 shallots, minced

2 garlic cloves, minced

1 tablespoon tomato paste

½ cup dry Marsala

½ cup dry red wine

2 tablespoons chopped fresh parsley

1 bay leaf

½ teaspoon fennel seeds, crushed

2 teaspoons cornstarch

Salt and freshly ground black pepper to taste

1. Preheat the oven broiler, and line a broiler pan with heavy-duty aluminum foil. Broil pork for 3 minutes per side, or until browned. Transfer pork to the slow cooker, and pour in any juices that have collected in the pan.

2. Heat oil in a small skillet over medium-high heat. Add shallots and garlic, and cook, stirring frequently, for 3 minutes, or until shallots are translucent. Scrape mixture into the slow cooker. Add tomato paste, Marsala, wine, parsley, bay leaf, and fennel seeds to the slow cooker, and stir well.

3. Cook on Low for 6 to 8 hours or on High for 3 to 4 hours, or until pork is tender. Remove and discard bay leaf. If cooking on Low, raise the heat to High. Mix cornstarch with 2 tablespoons cold water in a small cup. Add cornstarch mixture to the slow cooker, cover, and cook for an additional 10 to 15 minutes, or until the juices are bubbling and slightly thickened. Season to taste with salt and pepper, and serve hot.

Note: The dish can be prepared up to 2 days in advance and refrigerated, tightly covered. Reheat it, covered, over low heat until hot, stirring occasionally.

Variation:

✳ Substitute 1 (3- to 3¹/₂-pound) chicken, cut into serving pieces with the breast halves cut into 2 pieces, for the pork. Cook chicken on Low for 6 to 8 hours or on High for 3 to 4 hours or until chicken is cooked through, tender, and no longer pink.

All salt is not the same. Common table salt is finely ground and made with additives that prevent it from clumping. Iodized salt is table salt with added iodine to help prevent hypothyroidism in places lacking natural iodine. Kosher salt contains no additives and is coarse-grained. Some Jewish cooks use it ritualistically in meat preparation; many other cooks prefer it for its texture and flavor. At the top of the gourmet salt chain is sea salt, a product of evaporated sea water, available in finely-grained or larger crystals.

Pork Stew with Porcini and Juniper

While using juniper berries is common in Italy, it's so uncommon here that they are difficult to find. However, juniper is the primary flavor in gin, so that's an easy adjustment to make. This stew is also flavored with heady wild mushrooms and white wine.

Makes 4 to 6 servings | Active time: 20 minutes | Minimum cook time: 3¹/₄ hours in a medium slow cooker

1 ounce dried porcini mushrooms

1½ cups Chicken Stock (page 19) or purchased stock

2½ pounds country ribs, cut into 3-inch segments

2 tablespoons olive oil

1 large shallot, minced

2 garlic cloves, minced

½ cup dry white wine

2 tablespoons gin

2 anchovy fillets, minced

1 tablespoon chopped fresh marjoram

2 teaspoons cornstarch

Salt and freshly ground black pepper to taste

1. Combine porcini mushrooms and stock in a saucepan, and bring to a boil over high heat, stirring occasionally. Soak mushrooms for 10 minutes, pressing mushrooms down with the back of a spoon to keep them submerged. Drain mushrooms, reserving soaking liquid, and chop mushrooms. Strain soaking liquid through a sieve lined with a paper coffee filter or a paper towel. Set aside.

2. Preheat the oven broiler, and line a broiler pan with heavy-duty aluminum foil. Broil pork for 3 minutes per side, or until browned. Transfer pork to the slow cooker, and pour in any juices that have collected in the pan.

3. Heat oil in a small skillet over medium-high heat. Add shallot and garlic, and cook, stirring frequently, for 3 minutes, or until shallot is translucent. Scrape mixture into the slow cooker.

4. Add mushrooms and soaking liquid, wine, gin, anchovies, and marjoram to the slow cooker, and stir well. Cook on Low for 6 to 8 hours or on High for 3 to 4 hours, or until pork is tender.

5. If cooking on Low, raise the heat to High. Mix cornstarch and 2 tablespoons cold water in a small cup. Stir mixture into pork. Cook for an additional 15 to 20 minutes, or until juices are bubbling and slightly thickened. Season to taste with salt and pepper, and serve hot.

Note: The dish can be prepared up to 2 days in advance and refrigerated, tightly covered. Reheat it, covered, over low heat until hot, stirring occasionally.

Variation:

✳ Substitute 1 (3- to 3¹/₂-pound) chicken, cut into serving pieces with the breast halves cut into 2 pieces, for the pork. Cook chicken on Low for 6 to 8 hours or on High for 3 to 4 hours or until chicken is cooked through, tender, and no longer pink.

> Although the name actually means "little pigs" in Italian, porcini mushrooms are extremely flavorful and aromatic when dried. If you can't find porcini mushrooms, dried Polish mushrooms are a good substitute. Dried shiitake mushrooms do not have the same flavor, but they can be used in a pinch.

Pork Stew with Chestnuts

When I lived in Washington, DC, my favorite Italian restaurant was Galileo, headed up by talented chef Roberto Donna, a native of the Piedmont. This was one of his specialties, and in fall when chestnuts are fresh it can't be beaten.

Makes 4 to 6 servings | Active time: 20 minutes | Minimum cook time: 3½ hours in a medium slow cooker

1½ pounds boneless pork loin, cut into 1-inch cubes

2 tablespoons olive oil

1 medium onion, diced

1 carrot, diced

2 celery ribs, diced

2 tablespoons chopped fresh sage

2 cups dry red wine

½ cup Chicken Stock (page 19) or purchased stock

1 (3-inch) cinnamon stick

1 bay leaf

Pinch of ground cloves

1 (10-ounce) jar cooked chestnuts

2 teaspoons cornstarch

Salt and freshly ground black pepper to taste

1. Preheat the oven broiler, and line a broiler pan with heavy-duty aluminum foil. Broil pork for 3 minutes per side, or until browned. Transfer pork to the slow cooker, and pour in any juices that have collected in the pan.

2. Heat oil in a small skillet over medium-high heat. Add onion, carrot, celery, and sage, and cook, stirring frequently, for 3 minutes, or until onion is translucent. Scrape mixture into the slow cooker.

3. Add wine, stock, cinnamon stick, bay leaf, and cloves to the slow cooker, and stir well. Cook on Low for 6 to 8 hours or on High for 3 to 4 hours, or until pork is tender.

4. If cooking on Low, raise the heat to High. Mix cornstarch and 2 tablespoons cold water in a small cup. Stir chestnuts and cornstarch mixture into pork. Cook for an additional 15 to 20 minutes, or until juices are bubbling and slightly thickened. Remove and discard cinnamon stick and bay leaf, season to taste with salt and pepper, and serve hot.

Note: The dish can be prepared up to 2 days in advance and refrigerated, tightly covered. Reheat it, covered, over low heat until hot, stirring occasionally.

Variation:
✳ Substitute cubes of veal for the pork.

> To save time when making a recipe with many liquid ingredients, measure them into the same large cup, calculating what the level should be after each addition.

Chapter 8

Contorni

Vegetables, Legumes, and Grains as Side Dishes

The literal translation of *contorno*, or the plural of *contorni*, is "outline" or "border." It comes from the verb *contornare*, or "to surround." But used in its culinary form, what the *contorni* surround is the main course. They are the all-important side dishes that accompany an entrée. Those are the recipes you'll find in this chapter.

In Italian restaurants *contorni* are frequently ordered for the table of diners because unlike in other restaurants where the entrée plate is garnished by the chef with an appropriate combination of vegetables and carbohydrates, that does not happen often in Italy. So the side dishes become a category of their own, to be shared by diners regardless of what protein will be on their plates.

As is true with all recipes in this book, the side dishes emerging from the slow cooker are soft, not crisp-tender. But there is a wide range of vegetables that take well to braising, as well as bean dishes and grains. Each of these recipes have a character all their own too.

Basics for Dried Beans

Slow cookers are perfect for cooking beans and pulses; keep in mind that the slow cookers of today represent the evolution of the classic bean pot. The first step for all bean recipes is to rinse the beans in a sieve or colander, and look them over carefully to discard any broken beans or the occasional pebble that sneaks into the bag. Also, keep in mind when you're cooking beans to not fill the slow cooker more than one third with beans because they more than double in volume once they're cooked.

Although guidelines are given for how long each bean recipe takes to cook, there are variables that influence this time. If beans are a few years old, they'll take longer to cook. Also, the minerals in your tap water can retard the softening and require a longer cooking time, as can the addition of sweeteners such as maple syrup or acids such as tomatoes or wine.

Cooking beans is common sense; the larger the bean the longer it will take to soften. But it's not necessary to pre-soak larger beans for a longer period of time than smaller beans. There's only so much softening that goes on at no or low heat. Beans need to be gently simmered, and that's why the slow cooker is your best friend. It's far more patient than any pot on a stove to accomplish this task.

The chart is based on two cups of dried beans, which yields six cups of cooked beans.

Bean Cooking Chart

BEAN TYPE	TIME ON HIGH
Black beans	3 hours
Black-eyed peas	3 1/4 hours
Fava beans	2 3/4 hours
Garbanzo beans	3 1/2 hours
Great Northern beans	2 3/4 hours
Kidney beans	3 hours
Lentils	2 hours (no presoaking)
Lima beans	2 1/2 for baby, 3 1/2 for large
Navy beans	2 1/2 hours
Split peas	2 1/2 hours (no presoaking)
White beans	3 hours

Keep in mind that beans should always be covered with liquid at all times while they're cooking, so toward the end of the cooking process take a look and add boiling water if the water seems almost evaporated.

Mixed Vegetable Stew

This stew is similar to the ratatouille served in France; it contains a number of colorful vegetables as well as olives and capers for textural interest. Serve it with simple entrees to add color to the plate.

Makes 4 to 6 servings | Prep time: 20 minutes | Minimum cook time: 2¹/₂ hours in a medium slow cooker

1 (1-pound) eggplant

Salt

¹/₃ cup olive oil, divided

1 large onion, diced

3 garlic cloves, minced

2 red bell peppers, seeds and ribs removed, and thinly sliced

2 small zucchini, cut into ¾-inch cubes

1 small summer squash, cut into ¾-inch cubes

1 (14.5-ounce) can diced tomatoes, undrained

½ cup sliced green olives

1 cup Vegetable Stock (page 23) or purchased stock

2 tablespoons tomato paste

1 tablespoon chopped fresh oregano or 1 teaspoon dried

1 tablespoon fresh thyme or ½ teaspoon dried

1 tablespoon capers, drained and rinsed

Freshly ground black pepper to taste

1. Rinse and trim eggplant, and cut into ³/₄-inch cubes. Put eggplant in a colander, and sprinkle it liberally with salt. Place a plate on top of eggplant cubes, and weight the plate with cans. Place the colander in the sink or on a plate, and allow eggplant to drain for 30 minutes. Rinse eggplant cubes, and wring them dry with paper towels.

2. Heat half of oil in a medium skillet over medium-high heat. Add onion, garlic, and red bell peppers. Cook, stirring frequently, for 3 minutes, or until onion is translucent. Scrape mixture into the slow cooker.

3. Add remaining oil to the skillet, and add eggplant cubes. Cook, stirring frequently, for 3 minutes, or until eggplant begins to soften. Scrape eggplant into the slow cooker.

4. Add zucchini, summer squash, tomatoes, olives, stock, tomato paste, oregano, thyme, and capers to the slow cooker, and stir well. Cook on Low for 5 to 7 hours or on High for 2¹/₂ to 3¹/₂ hours, or until vegetables are tender. Season to taste with salt and pepper, and serve hot.

Note: The dish can be prepared up to 2 days in advance and refrigerated, tightly covered. Reheat it, covered, over low heat until hot, stirring occasionally.

Variation:

❋ Add 1 (15-ounce) can garbanzo beans or kidney beans, drained and rinsed, to the slow cooker in step 4 with the other additions.

There are two reasons why eggplant is salted before cooking. The first is to draw out the innate bitterness and the other is draw out some of the water so that it sautés more easily. While this is necessary with large eggplants, it can be skipped if using thin Japanese eggplants. That species isn't as bitter.

Tomato Pudding

This homey and comforting dish is like a combination of a gratin and a bread pudding. I love it in fall when the tomatoes are still wonderful but the evenings are chilly enough to enjoy them hot.

Makes 4 to 6 servings | Prep time: 15 minutes | Minimum cook time: 2 hours in a medium slow cooker

3 pounds ripe tomatoes

⅓ cup olive oil

4 garlic cloves, minced

¼ loaf Italian bread, cut into ½-inch cubes (about 3 cups)

2 teaspoons chopped fresh oregano or ½ teaspoon dried

1 teaspoon fresh thyme or ⅛ teaspoon dried

⅓ cup heavy cream

¼ cup freshly grated Parmesan cheese

Salt and freshly ground black pepper to taste

Vegetable oil spray

1. Grease the inside of the slow cooker liberally with vegetable oil spray. Rinse tomatoes and discard cores. Squeeze tomatoes to discard seeds, and cut tomatoes into ½-inch dice. Set aside.

2. Heat oil in a large skillet over medium-high heat. Add garlic and cook, stirring constantly, for 2 minutes. Add bread cubes, and cook for 3 to 4 minutes, stirring frequently, until cubes are lightly browned. Scrape mixture into the slow cooker.

3. Add tomatoes, oregano, thyme, cream, Parmesan cheese, salt, and pepper to the slow cooker. Toss to combine, and spread mixture evenly, patting it down with the back of a spoon. Cook on Low for 3 to 4 hours or on High for 2 to 3 hours, or until tomatoes are soft. Serve gratin hot.

Note: The dish can be prepared up to 2 days in advance and refrigerated, tightly covered. Reheat it, covered, in a 350°F oven for 20 to 25 minutes, or until hot.

Variation:
✳ Substitute olive bread or herb bread for the Italian bread.

> Markets today are drowning in olive oils in all price ranges. The expensive stuff is a condiment and is meant to be drizzled on salads. The cheap stuff is for cooking foods. Not only is it a waste of money to use expensive oil in cooking, but it also doesn't work as well.

Braised Radicchio

There are few dishes as pretty as radicchio on a plate. While braising dulls the color slightly from its shocking fuchsia, it's still vibrant, and the slightly bitter flavor is mellowed both by the herbs and a bit of sweet balsamic vinegar.

Makes 4 to 6 servings | Prep time: 10 minutes | Minimum cook time: 3 hours in a medium slow cooker

4 to 6 heads radicchio

4 tablespoons unsalted butter, melted

¾ cup Vegetable Stock (page 23) or purchased stock

2 tablespoons chopped fresh parsley

2 teaspoons fresh thyme or ¼ teaspoon dried

2 tablespoons balsamic vinegar

Salt and freshly ground black pepper to taste

1. Rinse radicchio and discard outer leaves. Cut in half, and discard core. Cut each half into 3 wedges. Arrange radicchio in the slow cooker.

2. Add butter, stock, parsley, thyme, and vinegar to the slow cooker, and toss well. Cook on Low for 6 to 8 hours or on High for 3 to 4 hours, or until radicchio is very soft. Season to taste with salt and pepper, and serve hot.

Note: The dish can be prepared up to 2 days in advance and refrigerated, tightly covered. Reheat it, covered, over low heat until hot, stirring occasionally.

Variation:

* Substitute Belgian endive for the radicchio. Trim the root end, and cut each head in half.

Radicchio (pronounced *rah-DEE-key-oh*) is a bright burgundy-colored lettuce with strong white ribs that is related to the chicory family. Native to Italy, radicchio comes in two types. Radicchio di Verona, what we find in American markets, grows in small, round heads. Radicchio di Treviso has tapered heads and grows in looser bunches.

Balsamic Onions

Onions are inherently sweet, and braising them in balsamic vinegar just accentuates this flavor element. Serve these with any bright and lightly colored secondi.

Makes 4 to 6 servings | Prep time: 10 minutes | Minimum cook time: 1¹/₂ hours in a medium slow cooker

1 (1-pound) package frozen pearl onions, thawed and drained

2 tablespoons unsalted butter, cut into small pieces

¼ cup balsamic vinegar

¼ cup Vegetable Stock (page 23) or purchased stock

2 tablespoons granulated sugar

2 teaspoons fresh thyme or ¼ teaspoon dried

Salt and freshly ground black pepper to taste

1. Put onions in the slow cooker, and dot top with butter pieces. Combine vinegar, stock, sugar, and thyme in a small bowl, and stir to dissolve sugar. Pour mixture over onions.

2. Cook on Low for 3 to 5 hours or on High for 1¹/₂ to 2 hours, or until onions are tender. Stir onions a few times after the liquid starts to simmer. Season to taste with salt and pepper, and serve hot.

Note: The dish can be prepared up to 2 days in advance and refrigerated, tightly covered. Reheat it, covered, over low heat until hot, stirring occasionally.

Variation:

* Substitute diced sweet onions, such as Vidalia or Bermuda, for the pearl onions, and increase the cooking time by 1¹/₂ hours on Low or 45 minutes on high.

Any cook who has slipped the skins off of a few pounds of pearl onions appreciates the treasure they are when finding them in the freezer case; it's a terrible job. However, you have to keep in mind that frozen onions are already partially cooked, which is why this dish has such a relatively short cooking time.

Braised Fennel

Fennel has an almost silky texture and sweet flavor once it's braised, and this dish is like a utility infielder in baseball; it goes with almost anything and everything, especially dishes with dark colors and assertive seasonings.

Makes 4 to 6 servings | Prep time: 10 minutes | Minimum cook time: 2 hours in a medium slow cooker

2 medium fennel bulbs, about 1 pound each

2 tablespoons unsalted butter

½ small onion, thinly sliced

1 garlic clove, minced

1 cup Vegetable Stock (page 23) or purchased stock

2 teaspoons fresh thyme or ¼ teaspoon dried

Salt and freshly ground black pepper to taste

1. Cut stalks off fennel bulb, trim root end, and cut bulb in half through the root. Trim out core, then slice fennel into 1-inch-thick slices across the bulb. Arrange slices in the slow cooker, and repeat with second bulb.

2. Heat butter in a small skillet over medium heat. Add onion and garlic, and cook, stirring frequently, for 3 minutes, or until onion is translucent. Scrape mixture into the slow cooker.

3. Add stock and thyme to the slow cooker. Cook on Low for 4 to 6 hours or on High for 2 to 3 hours, or until fennel is tender. Season to taste with salt and pepper, and serve hot.

Note: The dish can be prepared up to 2 days in advance and refrigerated, tightly covered. Reheat it, covered, over low heat until hot, stirring occasionally.

Variation:
* Substitute celery ribs for the fennel.

> **Although the celery-like stalks are trimmed off the fennel bulb for this dish, don't throw them out. They add a wonderful anise flavor as well as a crisp texture and are used in place of celery in salads and other raw dishes.**

Broccoli with Red Wine

While this dish is served in many parts of Italy, most food historians believe it is native to Sicily. The broccoli is cooked with olives and anchovies in red wine, and then some cheese finishes the dish.

Makes 6 to 8 servings | *Prep time: 15 minutes* | *Minimum cook time: 2¹/₂ hours in a medium slow cooker*

1½ pounds broccoli crowns

⅓ cup olive oil

1 large onion, diced

¾ cup dry red wine

8 anchovy fillets, finely chopped

3 tablespoons chopped fresh parsley

⅓ cup chopped pitted brine-cured black olives

¾ cup grated sharp provolone cheese

Freshly ground black pepper to taste

1. Rinse broccoli and break into florets. Heat olive oil in a large skillet over medium-high heat. Add onion and broccoli and cook, stirring frequently, for 3 minutes, or until onion is translucent. Scrape mixture into the slow cooker.

2. Add wine, anchovies, parsley, and olives to the slow cooker, and stir well. Cook on Low for 4 to 6 hours or on High for 2 to 3 hours, or until broccoli is tender.

3. If cooking on Low, raise the heat to High. Stir in cheese, and cook for 15 to 30 minutes, or until cheese melts. Season to taste with pepper, and serve hot.

Note: The dish can be prepared up to 2 days in advance and refrigerated, tightly covered. Reheat it, covered, in a 350°F oven for 20 to 25 minutes, or until hot.

Variation:

∗ Substitute cauliflower for the broccoli and substitute white wine for the red wine.

When we think about vitamin C, citrus fruits usually come to mind. But a serving of broccoli contains more than 200 percent of the RDA for vitamin C. No wonder it's considered a "wonder food."

Leeks Gratinée

Leeks are the mildest of the onion family, as well as the most elegant. And this is one of the most elegant ways to serve them, topped with a crispy crust of cheese and breadcrumbs after being braised in the slow cooker.

Makes 4 to 6 servings | Prep time: 15 minutes | Minimum cook time: 2 hours in a medium slow cooker

12 to 18 small leeks

2 tablespoons unsalted butter, melted

⅓ cup Vegetable Stock (page 23) or purchased stock

¼ cup dry white wine

2 tablespoons chopped fresh marjoram or 2 teaspoons dried

Salt and freshly ground black pepper to taste

½ cup plain breadcrumbs

½ cup grated fontina

½ cup freshly grated Parmesan cheese

1. Trim off root end of leeks and discard all but 1 inch of green tops. Split leeks lengthwise, and rinse well under cold running water, rubbing with your fingers to dislodge all grit. Arrange leeks in the slow cooker.

2. Add butter, stock, wine, and marjoram to the slow cooker. Cook on Low for 4 to 5 hours or on High for 2 to 2½ hours, or until leeks are tender.

3. Preheat the oven to 400°F. Remove leeks from the slow cooker with a slotted spatula and arrange them in a 9 x 13-inch pan. Season to taste with salt and pepper. Combine breadcrumbs, fontina, and Parmesan in a bowl, and sprinkle mixture on top of leeks.

4. Bake leeks for 15 minutes, or until top is browned. Serve immediately.

Note: The leeks can be cooked up to 2 days in advance and refrigerated, tightly covered. Do the final baking just prior to serving.

Variation:

✽ Substitute 3 bunches of scallions, white parts and 4 inches of green tops, for the leeks. Decrease the cooking time by 1 hour on Low or 30 minutes on High.

> Grating cheese is a snap in a food processor fitted with a steel blade. If you're doing it by hand with a box grater, spray the grater with vegetable oil spray and the cheese will grate far more easily.

Carrots with Vermouth

This dish is traditionally made with sweet Marsala, which can be used as a substitute, but I like it better with the more assertive flavor of sweet vermouth. It gives the carrots a blushing bright color too.

Makes 6 to 8 servings | Prep time: 10 minutes | Minimum cook time: 3 hours in a medium slow cooker

2 pounds peeled baby carrots

3 tablespoons unsalted butter, melted

½ cup sweet vermouth

¼ cup Vegetable Stock (page 23) or purchased stock

Salt and freshly ground black pepper to taste

2 tablespoons chopped fresh parsley

1. Combine carrots, butter, vermouth, and vegetable stock in the slow cooker, and stir well.

2. Cook on Low for 6 to 8 hours or on High for 3 to 4 hours, or until carrots are tender. Season to taste with salt and pepper, remove carrots from the slow cooker with a slotted spoon, and serve hot, sprinkling each serving with parsley.

Note: The dish can be prepared up to 2 days in advance and refrigerated, tightly covered. Reheat it, covered, over low heat until hot, stirring occasionally.

Variation:

* Substitute 1 pound parsnips for 1 pound of the carrots. Peel the turnips and cut them into rectangles the same size as the carrots.

> Fortified wines like vermouth, Port, and Madiera do not need to be refrigerated after opening the bottle. However, they will not age more once the contents have been exposed to oxygen.

Potatoes with Herbs

While most of the potatoes served in Italy are simply prepared, I'm very fond of this treatment to add extra flavors to the spuds. They are combined with onions and herbs and then cooked in stock.

Makes 6 to 8 servings | Prep time: 15 minutes | Minimum cook time: 3 hours in a medium slow cooker

2½ pounds Yukon gold potatoes, peeled and cut into chunks

2 medium onions, thinly sliced

2 garlic cloves, minced

3 tablespoons unsalted butter, cut into small pieces

2 tablespoons chopped fresh parsley

1 tablespoon chopped fresh rosemary or 1 teaspoon dried

1½ teaspoons fresh thyme or ¼ teaspoon dried

1½ cups Chicken Stock (page 19) or purchased stock

Salt and freshly ground black pepper to taste

Vegetable oil spray

1. Spray the inside of the slow cooker liberally with vegetable oil spray. Combine potatoes, onion, garlic, butter, parsley, rosemary, and thyme in the slow cooker. Pack it down evenly. Pour stock over potatoes.

2. Cook on Low for 6 to 8 hours or on High for 3 to 4 hours, or until potatoes are tender. Season to taste with salt and pepper, and serve hot.

Note: The dish can be prepared up to 2 days in advance and refrigerated, tightly covered. Reheat it, covered, in a 350°F oven for 20 to 25 minutes, or until hot.

Variations:

✳ For a Sicilian variation, add 3 tablespoons capers, drained and rinsed, to the slow cooker.

✳ Add ½ to ¾ cup grated Gruyère to the slow cooker for the last 15 minutes of cooking time.

> If you're cooking potatoes in a slow cooker on Low, they might discolor. A way to avoid this is to submerge the potatoes in a bowl of water to which lemon juice has been added before cooking them. The lemon will not be detected once the dish is cooked, and it will keep the spuds snowy white.

Sardinian-Style Cabbage

This cabbage dish is subtly flavored with pancetta and herbs, and the braising makes it a tender treat for any winter meal.

Makes 6 to 8 servings | Prep time: 15 minutes | Minimum cook time: 2¹/₂ hours in a medium slow cooker

2 tablespoons olive oil

¼ pound pancetta, diced

2 garlic cloves, minced

1 (1½-pound) head green cabbage, shredded

2 tablespoons fresh chopped parsley

1 bay leaf

1 cup Chicken Stock (page 19) or purchased stock

Salt and freshly ground black pepper to taste

1. Heat oil in a large skillet over medium-high heat. Add pancetta, stirring frequently, and cook for 4 to 5 minutes, or until browned. Add garlic, and cook for 30 seconds, stirring constantly. Add cabbage, parsley, bay leaf, and stock, and bring to a boil. Scrape mixture into the slow cooker.

2. Cook on Low for 5 to 7 hours or on High for 2 ¹/₂ to 3 hours, or until cabbage softens. Remove and discard bay leaf, season to taste with salt and pepper, and serve hot.

Note: The dish can be prepared up to 2 days in advance and refrigerated, tightly covered. Reheat it, covered, in a 350°F oven for 20 to 25 minutes, or until hot.

Variation:

✳ Substitute red cabbage for the green cabbage if you want more color on the plate.

An advantage of cooking *cruciferous* vegetables such as cabbage, cauliflower, or broccoli in the slow cooker is that the house doesn't smell like vegetables for days, which many people find offensive. This is because very little liquid evaporates from the slow cooker, and it's the steam in the air that carries the "fragrance."

Beans with Tomatoes and Sage

Sage is a great herb, although in this country we seem to relegate it to inclusion in Thanksgiving stuffing. It melds wonderfully with the beans and tomatoes in this Tuscan version of a classic bean dish.

Makes 6 to 8 servings | Prep time: 15 minutes | Minimum cook time: 2¹/₂ hours in a medium slow cooker

1 pound dried cannellini beans

2 teaspoons salt

¼ cup olive oil

1 large shallot, minced

3 garlic cloves, minded

¼ cup chopped fresh sage

1 (14.5-ounce) can diced tomatoes, undrained

3 to 4 cups Vegetable Stock (page 23) or purchased stock

Salt and freshly ground black pepper to taste

1. Rinse beans in a colander and place them in a mixing bowl covered with 1 quart cold water mixed with salt. Allow beans to soak for at least six hours, or overnight. Or place beans into a saucepan with water and salt, and bring to a boil over high heat. Boil 1 minute. Turn off the heat, cover the pan, and soak beans for 1 hour. With either soaking method, drain beans, discard soaking water, and begin cooking as soon as possible.

2. Heat oil in a small skillet over medium-high heat. Add shallot and garlic, and cook, stirring frequently, for 3 minutes, or until shallot is translucent. Scrape mixture into the slow cooker.

3. Add drained beans, sage, and tomatoes to the slow cooker. Add enough stock to cover beans by 1 inch. Stir well. Cook on Low for 5 to 7 hours or on High for 2¹/₂ to 3 hours, or until beans are tender. Season to taste with salt and pepper, and serve hot.

Note: The dish can be prepared up to 2 days in advance and refrigerated, tightly covered. Reheat it, covered, in a 350°F oven for 20 to 25 minutes, or until hot.

Variation:

✳ Add ¹/₂ cup diced prosciutto and ¹/₄ cup chopped brine-cured black olives to the slow cooker along with the beans.

Although many dried beans can be substituted for one another, don't substitute with canned beans in the slow cooker. Canned beans are already fully cooked, and they'll fall apart before they absorb the flavoring from the slow-cooked dish.

Kidney Bean and Roasted Garlic Puree

Vegetables purees are at the center of classic French cooking, but they are not as popular in Italy. One exception however, are silky smooth bean purees, and this one is augmented by the nutty sweetness of roasted garlic.

Makes 6 to 8 servings | Prep time: 20 minutes | Minimum cook time: 3 hours in a medium slow cooker

1½ cups dried kidney beans

2 teaspoons salt

5 cups Vegetable Stock (page 23) or purchased stock

1 medium onion, halved through the root end

3 garlic cloves, minced

1 bay leaf

Salt and freshly ground black pepper to taste

4 heads Roasted Garlic (page 47), cloves removed

¼ cup olive oil

1. Rinse beans in a colander and place them in a mixing bowl covered with 1 quart cold water mixed with salt. Allow beans to soak for at least six hours, or overnight. Or place beans into a saucepan with water and salt, and bring to a boil over high heat. Boil 1 minute. Turn off the heat, cover the pan, and soak beans for 1 hour. With either soaking method, drain beans, discard soaking water, and begin cooking as soon as possible.

2. Add drained beans, stock, onion, garlic, and bay leaf to the slow cooker. Cook on Low for 6 to 8 hours or on High for 3 to 4 hours, or until beans are tender. Add salt and pepper prior to the last hour of cooking time. Remove and discard onion and bay leaf.

3. Drain beans, reserving 1 cup of cooking liquid. Remove pulp from roasted garlic, and discard skins. Combine garlic with ½ cup cooking liquid in a food processor fitted with a steel blade or a blender. Puree until smooth. Add beans and puree until smooth, adding more cooking liquid if necessary. Drizzle olive oil through the feed tube. Season to taste with salt and pepper, and serve hot.

Note: The dish can be prepared up to 2 days in advance and refrigerated, tightly covered. Reheat it, covered, in a 350°F oven for 20 to 25 minutes, or until hot.

Variations:

* Substitute cannellini beans or garbanzo beans for the kidney beans. Add 1 hour of cooking time on Low or 30 minutes of cooking time on High if cooking garbanzo beans.

* Add ½ to 1 teaspoon crushed red pepper flakes to the slow cooker for a spicier dish.

Garlic is native to Asia Minor, so it's not surprising that the ancient Egyptians worshiped garlic and placed clay models of garlic bulbs in the tomb of Tutankhamen. Garlic was so highly prized it was even used as currency.

Garbanzo Bean Stew

This is a hearty winter bean stew. The nutty garbanzo beans are cooked in tomato juice with herbs and seasonings, and then some cheeses are added to create a creamy sauce.

Makes 4 to 6 servings | Prep time: 15 minutes | Minimum cook time: 5 1/2 hours in a medium slow cooker

1½ cups dried garbanzo beans

2 teaspoons salt

2 tablespoons olive oil

1 medium onion, diced

3 garlic cloves, minced

½ orange bell pepper, seeds and ribs removed, and finely chopped

2 cups tomato juice

1 (14.5-ounce) can diced tomatoes, undrained

3 tablespoons chopped fresh parsley

1 tablespoon fresh chopped marjoram or 1 teaspoon dried

1 bay leaf

½ cup grated whole-milk mozzarella cheese

¼ cup freshly grated Parmesan cheese

Salt and freshly ground black pepper to taste

1. Rinse beans in a colander and place them in a mixing bowl covered with 1 quart cold water mixed with salt. Allow beans to soak for at least six hours, or overnight. Or place beans into a saucepan with water and salt, and bring to a boil over high heat. Boil 1 minute. Turn off the heat, cover the pan, and soak beans for 1 hour. With either soaking method, drain beans, discard soaking water, and begin cooking as soon as possible.

2. Heat oil in a medium skillet over medium-high heat. Add onion, garlic, and bell pepper. Cook, stirring frequently, for 3 minutes, or until onion is translucent. Scrape mixture into the slow cooker.

3. Add drained beans, tomato juice, tomatoes, parsley, marjoram, and bay leaf to the slow cooker, and stir well. Cook on Low for 10 to 12 hours or on High for 5 to 6 hours, or until beans are tender.

4. If cooking on Low, raise the heat to High. Remove and discard bay leaf, stir in mozzarella and Parmesan cheeses, and season to taste with salt and pepper. Cook for 10 to 15 minutes, or until cheeses melt. Serve immediately.

Note: The dish can be prepared up to 2 days in advance and refrigerated, tightly covered. Reheat it, covered, in a 350°F oven for 20 to 25 minutes, or until hot.

Variation:

✳ Substitute cannellini beans or kidney beans for the garbanzo beans, and cut 2 hours off the cooking time on Low or 1 hour on High.

Marjoram (pronounced *MAHR-jur-umm*) is a member of the mint family. The flavor from the long, pale-green leaves is similar to that of oregano but sweeter. If you can't find marjoram, use oregano, but use only half as much as you would marjoram.

Cauliflower with Raisins and Pine Nuts

In Italy this dish is made with a bright chartreuse vegetable we call broccoflower, which is also called Romanesco broccoli. It's becoming more available at upscale supermarkets and specialty produce markets, but plain old snowy white cauliflower works just fine. The combination of sweet raisins and crunchy pine nuts elevate this simple dish to elegance.

Makes 6 to 8 servings | Prep time: 15 minutes | Minimum cook time: 2 hours in a medium slow cooker

1 (1½-pound) head cauliflower

¼ cup olive oil, divided

2 garlic cloves, minced

¼ cup raisins

½ cup Vegetable Stock (page 23) or purchased stock

3 tablespoons pine nuts

2 tablespoons chopped fresh parsley

Salt and freshly ground black pepper to taste

1. Discard leaves and core from cauliflower, and cut into 1-inch florets. Transfer cauliflower to the slow cooker.

2. Heat 2 tablespoons oil in a small skillet over medium-high heat. Add garlic, and cook for 30 seconds, or until fragrant. Scrape garlic into the slow cooker, add raisins and stock, and stir well. Cook for Low for 4 to 6 hours or on High for 2 to 3 hours, or until cauliflower is tender.

3. While cauliflower cooks, heat remaining oil in the skillet over medium heat. Add pine nuts, and cook for 2 minutes, or until brown. Set aside.

4. Remove cauliflower from the slow cooker with a slotted spoon, and toss with pine nuts and parsley. Season to taste with salt and pepper, and serve hot.

Note: The dish can be prepared up to 2 days in advance without adding the pine nuts and parsley, and refrigerated, tightly covered. Reheat it, covered, in a 350°F oven for 20 to 25 minutes, or until hot, before tossing with the nuts and parsley.

Variation:

✳ Substitute broccoli for the cauliflower. The cooking time will remain the same.

Toast small nuts and seeds, such as pine nuts, sesame seeds, and slivered almonds, in a small dry skillet over medium-high heat. Toast larger nuts such as pecans, walnuts, or whole almonds, in the oven.

Farro with Fennel

The slight anise flavor of fennel is wonderful to enhance the heartiness of farro, and the carrot adds color.

Makes 4 to 6 servings | Prep time: 15 minutes | Minimum cook time: 2¹/₂ hours in a medium slow cooker

3 tablespoons unsalted butter

1 small onion, finely chopped

¹/₂ fennel bulb, cored and thinly sliced

¹/₂ carrot, diced

1¹/₂ cup farro

2¹/₂ cups Vegetable Stock (page 23) or purchased stock

1 tablespoon fresh thyme or ¹/₂ teaspoon dried

Salt and freshly ground black pepper to taste

1. Melt butter in a medium skillet over medium-high heat. Add onion, fennel, and carrot. Cook, stirring frequently, for 3 minutes, or until onion is translucent. Scrape mixture into the slow cooker.

2. Add farro, stock, and thyme to the slow cooker. Cook on Low for 5 to 7 hours or on High for 2¹/₂ to 3 hours, or until farro is plump and tender and liquid is absorbed. Season to taste with salt and pepper, and serve immediately.

Note: The dish can be prepared up to 2 days in advance and refrigerated, tightly covered. Reheat it, covered, in a 350°F oven for 20 to 25 minutes, or until hot.

Variation:

＊ Stir ¹/₂ cup freshly grated Parmesan cheese to the farro before seasoning it with salt and pepper.

> Farro, sometimes called *spelt*, is an ancient grain native to southern Europe. It has a mellow, nutty flavor and is easily digestible. It contains more protein than wheat, and it's sometimes ground into flour.

Farro Pilaf

There's a nutty richness to farro, an up-and-coming grain in the bulk bin department of whole foods markets. This simple preparation with vegetables amplifies this quality. Serve this with almost anything that has assertive flavors so that it will balance rather than overwhelm it.

Makes 4 to 6 servings | Prep time: 20 minutes | Minimum cook time: 2¹/₂ hours in a medium slow cooker

3 tablespoons olive oil

1 medium onion, chopped

1 red bell pepper, seeds and ribs removed, and chopped

1 celery rib, chopped

3 garlic cloves, minced

1½ cups farro, rinsed

2½ cups Vegetable Stock (page 23) or purchased stock

1 (14.5-ounce) can diced tomatoes, undrained

½ cup oil-cured black olives

1 tablespoon fresh thyme or ½ teaspoon dried

1 bay leaf

Salt and freshly ground black pepper to taste

3 tablespoons chopped fresh parsley

1. Heat olive oil in a large skillet over medium-high heat. Add onion, red bell pepper, celery, and garlic. Cook, stirring frequently, for 3 minutes, or until onion is translucent. Scrape mixture into the slow cooker.

2. Add farro, stock, tomatoes, olives, thyme, and bay leaf to the slow cooker, and stir well. Cook on Low for 5 to 7 hours or on High for 2¹/₂ to 3 hours, or until farro is plump and tender and liquid is absorbed.

3. Remove and discard bay leaf. Season to taste with salt and pepper, stir in parsley, and serve hot.

Note: The dish can be prepared up to 2 days in advance and refrigerated, tightly covered. Reheat it, covered, in a 350°F oven for 20 to 25 minutes, or until hot.

Variation:
✷ Substitute wheat berries or bulgur for the farro.

Pilaf (pronounced *PEE-laf*) is used in our culture for almost any grain dish that includes other ingredients, such as the vegetables and is cooked in stock rather than water. Pilaf originated in the Middle East where it was always made with rice or bulgur wheat, which were browned before any liquid was added.

Toasted Barley with Mushrooms

Barley, an ancient grain, is served more often in northern Italy than in the southern provinces. The addition of mushrooms and herbs augment the delicate flavor of the grain.

Makes 4 to 6 servings | Prep time: 15 minutes | Minimum cook time: 2 hours in a medium slow cooker

1 cup pearl barley

3 tablespoons unsalted butter

1 tablespoon olive oil

1 shallot, minced

½ pound white mushrooms, wiped with a damp paper towel, trimmed, and sliced

2 cups Vegetable Stock (page 23) or purchased stock

2 teaspoons fresh thyme or ¼ teaspoon dried

1 bay leaf

Salt and freshly ground black pepper to taste

1. Place a medium skillet over medium-high heat. Add barley and cook, stirring frequently, for 3 to 5 minutes, or until barley is lightly toasted. Transfer barley to the slow cooker.

2. Add butter and oil to the skillet. When butter melts, add shallot and mushrooms. Cook, stirring frequently, for 3 to 5 minutes, or until mushrooms begin to soften. Scrape mixture into the slow cooker.

3. Add stock, thyme, and bay leaf to the slow cooker, and stir well. Cook on Low for 4 to 6 hours or on High for 2 to 3 hours, or until barley is soft. Season to taste with salt and pepper, and serve hot.

Note: The dish can be prepared up to 2 days in advance and refrigerated, tightly covered. Reheat it, covered, in a 350°F oven for 20 to 25 minutes, or until hot.

Variation:

＊ Substitute diced portobello mushrooms for the white mushrooms, and add 2 tablespoons chopped dried mushrooms to the slow cooker.

Toasting grains is an additional step for many recipes, but the results are worth it. Toasting cooks the starch on the exterior of the grain so the dish doesn't become gummy from too much starch when it cooks. Although barley is best toasted dry, any species of rice can be toasted in butter or oil. With rice, the grains just need to become opaque. They don't even have to brown.

Bulgur with Dried Fruit and Toasted Pine Nuts

Sweet dried fruits and vegetables flavor this cinnamon-scented grain side dish. It goes very well with poultry and pork secondi.

Makes 4 to 6 servings | Prep time: 20 minutes | Minimum cook time: 2 hours in a medium slow cooker

2 tablespoons olive oil

1 small onion, chopped

1 garlic clove, peeled and minced

1 cup medium or coarse bulgur

1½ cups Vegetable Stock (page 23) or purchased stock

1 large carrot, thickly sliced

¾ cup chopped dried figs, stemmed if necessary

1 (1-inch) cinnamon stick

½ cup pine nuts

Salt and freshly ground black pepper to taste

3 scallions, rinsed, trimmed, and chopped

1. Heat olive oil in a small skillet over medium-high heat. Add onion and garlic, and cook, stirring frequently, for 3 minutes, or until onion is translucent. Scrape mixture into the slow cooker.

2. Add bulgur, stock, carrots, figs, and cinnamon stick to the slow cooker, and stir well. Cook on Low for 4 to 6 hours or on High for 2 to 3 hours, or until liquid is absorbed.

3. While bulgur cooks, place pine nuts in a small dry skillet over medium heat. Toast pine nuts, shaking the pan frequently, for 3 minutes, or until browned. Set aside.

4. Remove and discard cinnamon stick. To serve, season to taste with salt and pepper, sprinkle each serving with pine nuts and scallions, and serve hot.

Note: The dish can be prepared up to 2 days in advance and refrigerated, tightly covered. Reheat it, covered, in a 350°F oven for 20 to 25 minutes, or until hot.

Variation:

∗ Substitute dried apricots or raisins for the dried figs.

Bulgur (pronounced *BULL-gurr*) is a wheat kernel that has been steamed, dried, and crushed. It's similar to cracked wheat and can be used in the same way. It has a chewy texture and comes both coarse and fine. Grains such as bulgur are dried but can spoil if they become too moist. It's important to store them in an airtight container in a dry place, or keep them frozen.

Chapter 9

Dolci

The Sweet Ending

The range of slow cooker desserts is limited, there's no doubt about it. The slow cooker cannot produce what pastry chefs define as an authentic cake. Cakes need the dry heat of an oven, and they need a higher temperature than that generated by a slow cooker, even one set on High. But what *can* be created are delicious dishes that are technically baked puddings but have the dry texture of a cake.

That's why the batters for the cake recipes in this chapter are much thicker than those for conventional cakes, because batters baking in a hot oven release moisture into the oven as they bake; they need to "dry out." The reverse is true for slow-cooker cakes. The steam generated by the cooking process becomes part of the cake and moistens it as it cooks.

Puddings of all types, not just ones masquerading as cakes, are perfect slow-cooker options because they need low heat. So you'll have bread puddings that are tender because the eggs can set and cook without becoming tough and rice puddings that are meltingly creamy because there's no fear that the rice will scorch.

The slow cooker is also a great appliance for poached and stewed fruits, which are very typical Italian desserts. Those recipes are at the end of the chapter, and all of these dishes are a great excuse to bring out a bottle of well-chilled vin santo.

Fig and Almond Cake

Dried figs are one of the most wonderful fruits on the market because their color and taste is so close to that of a fresh fig when cooked. For this cake the figs and crunchy nuts are moistened with a spiced sugar syrup before serving.

Makes 4 to 6 servings | Prep time: 20 minutes | Minimum cook time: 2 1/2 hours in a medium slow cooker

1½ cups slivered blanched almonds

¾ chopped dried figs, stems discarded if necessary

¼ cup grappa or brandy

1½ cups all-purpose flour

2 cups granulated sugar, divided

1¾ teaspoons baking powder

Pinch salt

3 large eggs, at room temperature

6 tablespoons unsalted butter, melted

1 (3-inch) cinnamon stick

2 (3-inch) strips lemon zest

Vegetable oil spray

Parchment paper

1. Preheat the oven to 350°F, and line a baking sheet with aluminum foil. Place almonds on the baking sheet and toast nuts for 5 to 7 minutes, or until browned. Set aside. Place figs in a small mixing bowl, and sprinkle with grappa. Set aside.

2. Using the bottom of the slow cooker insert as a guide, cut out a piece of parchment paper. Grease the inside of the slow cooker liberally with vegetable oil spray or butter. Place the parchment paper into the bottom, and grease it liberally as well.

3. Combine flour, ½ cup sugar, baking powder, and salt in a mixing bowl. Whisk eggs in another bowl, and add melted butter.

4. Add egg mixture to dry ingredients, and stir well. Add toasted nuts and figs. Stir well again, scrape batter into prepared slow cooker, and even out the top with a rubber spatula.

5. Cook cake on High for 2¼ to 2½ hours, or until a toothpick inserted in the center comes out clean. Turn off the slow cooker, remove the lid, and allow cake to cool for 15 minutes. Run a spatula around the edge of the insert, and then invert cake onto a serving platter.

6. While cake cooks, make syrup. Combine remaining 1½ cups sugar, 1 cup water, cinnamon stick, and lemon zest in a small saucepan. Bring to a boil over medium-high heat, stirring occasionally. Reduce the heat to low, and cook syrup for 10 minutes, stirring occasionally. Remove and discard cinnamon stick and lemon zest. To serve, cut cake into slices and drizzle syrup over each slice. Serve cake hot or at room temperature.

Note: The cake and syrup can both be prepared up to 2 days in advance and kept separately at room temperature, tightly covered with plastic wrap.

Variations:

* Substitute chopped walnuts for the almonds.
* Substitute chopped dried apricots or chopped dates for the figs.

Grappa is an Italian brandy made by distilling the skins, pulp, seeds, and stems from grapes what are leftover after making wine. Its flavor depends on the species of grape, and the name is now protected by the European Union. In France, the closest drink to grappa is marc.

Chocolate Pudding Cake

Italians love chocolate as much as Americans, and this dessert is a slow cooker adaptation of Bounet, a traditional pudding made with crushed amaretti cookies. It is native to the Piedmont region.

Makes 4 to 6 servings | Active time: 15 minutes | Minimum cook time: 2 hours in a medium slow cooker

1 cup granulated sugar

1 cup all-purpose flour

¾ cup crushed amaretti cookies

3 tablespoons plus ¼ cup unsweetened cocoa powder

2 teaspoons baking powder

⅓ cup whole milk

3 tablespoons unsalted butter, melted

2 tablespoons Amaretto or other almond liqueur

½ teaspoon pure almond extract

¾ cup firmly packed dark brown sugar

1¾ cups boiling water

Gelato or ice cream (optional)

Vegetable oil spray

1. Grease the inside of the slow cooker liberally with vegetable oil spray or melted butter. Combine granulated sugar, flour, crushed cookies, 3 tablespoons cocoa powder, and baking powder in a mixing bowl. Stir in milk, melted butter, Amaretto, and almond extract. Stir until stiff batter forms. Spread batter into the slow cooker.

2. Sprinkle brown sugar and remaining ¼ cup cocoa powder over the batter. Pour boiling water over the batter. Cook on High for 2 to 2¼ hours, or until a toothpick inserted into the top cake layer comes out clean. Allow cake to sit for 15 minutes with slow cooker turned off before serving.

Note: The cake can be served hot, at room temperature, or chilled, topped with gelato or ice cream, if using.

Variations:

✱ Add 1 tablespoon instant espresso granules to the batter for a mocha cake.

✱ Substitute Frangelico for the Amaretto and hazelnuts for the almonds.

✱ Add ¼ cup fruit-only jam to the batter for added flavor.

> Cocoa powder has a tendency to clump if exposed to humidity. The best way to handle this is to sift it before using it. If the clumps are large, you can also whir it in a food processor fitted with the steel blade.

Apple-Raisin Pudding Cake

This pudding cake is fairly light, and it delivers an intense apple flavor from three forms of the fruit. It's almost like an apple cobbler, with a thick sauce topping it.

Makes 4 to 6 servings | Active time: 15 minutes | Minimum cook time: 2 hours in a medium slow cooker

2 cups apple cider or apple juice

2 Granny Smith apples

1 cup all-purpose flour

¾ cup granulated sugar, divided

1 teaspoon baking powder

¼ teaspoon freshly grated nutmeg

Pinch of salt

½ cup whole milk

4 tablespoons (½ stick) unsalted butter, melted

¼ teaspoon pure vanilla extract

⅓ cup finely chopped dried apples

⅓ cup raisins

½ cup firmly packed dark brown sugar

Gelato or sweetened whipped cream (optional)

Vegetable oil spray

1. Bring apple cider to a boil in a small saucepan over high heat. Cook until cider is reduced by half. Set aside. Grease the inside of the slow cooker liberally with vegetable oil spray or melted butter.

2. While cider boils, peel and core apples, and chop apples finely in a food processor fitted with a steel blade using on-and-off pulsing. Combine flour, ⅓ cup granulated sugar, baking powder, nutmeg, and salt in a mixing bowl. Stir in milk, melted butter, and vanilla. Stir until a stiff batter forms, then stir in apples, dried apples, raisins, and brown sugar. Spread batter into the slow cooker.

3. Bring cider back to a boil, and stir in remaining sugar. Pour mixture over batter. Cook on High for 2 to 2¼ hours, or until a toothpick inserted into the top cake layer comes out clean. Turn off the slow cooker and remove the cover. Allow cake to sit for 15 minutes before serving.

Note: The cake can be served hot, at room temperature, or chilled, topped with gelato or whipped cream, if using.

Variation:

✳ Substitute 3 ripe peaches, peeled; dried peaches; and peach nectar for the various forms of apple in the recipe.

> Vegetable oil spray has a tendency to coat the counter as well as the inside of the slow cooker, so here's a trick to contain it: Open the dishwasher door, place the slow cooker insert right on the door, and spray away. Any excess or overspray will be cleaned off the door the next time you run the dishwasher.

Apple Bread Pudding

This rich and luscious bread pudding is based on a dish called *La Miaschi*a, which is served in homes on the shores of Lake Como. It's moist and contains succulent dried figs as well as apples.

Makes 6 to 8 servings | *Prep time: 20 minutes* | *Minimum cook time: 2¹/₂ hours in a medium slow cooker*

12 ounces stale bread, cut into 1-inch cubes

1½ pounds Granny Smith or Golden Delicious apples, peeled, cored, and chopped

¾ cup thinly sliced dried figs, stemmed if necessary

4 large eggs, lightly beaten

1 (14-ounce) can sweetened condensed milk

4 tablespoons (½ stick) unsalted butter, melted

2 tablespoons freshly squeezed lemon juice

2 teaspoons grated lemon zest

Pinch of salt

Pinch of freshly grated nutmeg

Gelato or sweetened whipped cream (optional)

Vegetable oil spray

1. Grease the inside of the slow cooker liberally with vegetable oil spray. Combine bread cubes, apples, and figs in the slow cooker. Combine eggs, condensed milk, melted butter, lemon juice, lemon zest, salt, and nutmeg, and whisk well. Pour mixture into the slow cooker, and stir well.

2. Cook on Low for 5 to 6 hours or on High for 2¹/₂ to 3 hours, or until the pudding is set and puffed. Serve pudding hot or warm, topped with gelato or whipped cream, if using.

Note: The dish can be prepared up to 2 days in advance and refrigerated, tightly covered. Reheat it, covered, in a 350°F oven for 20 to 25 minutes, or until hot.

Variations:
* Substitute ripe pears or apricots for the apples.
* Substitute raisins or chopped dried dates for the figs.

If it matters how the apples in the dish look, the time-honored way of peeling, coring, and then slicing each half or quarter is still the best method. But if the apples are going to be hidden, there's a faster way: Peel the apple and keep turning it in your hand as you cut off slices. Soon all you'll be left with is the core, which you can discard.

Panettone Bread Pudding

Panettone (pronounced *pan-uh-TOE-knee*) is a sweet yeast bread that originated in Milan. It usually contains some sort of raisins or other dried fruit, as well as some candied citrus peel. It is traditionally served at Christmas, as is this pudding made with it.

Makes 6 to 8 servings | Prep time: 25 minutes | Minimum cook time: 3 hours in a medium slow cooker

3 large eggs

1 cup granulated sugar

1¾ cups whole milk

6 tablespoons unsalted butter, melted

½ teaspoon pure vanilla extract

¼ teaspoon ground cinnamon

Pinch of salt

5 cups cubed panettone

½ cup golden raisins

¾ cup mixed candied fruits

Vegetable oil spray

Gelato or sweetened whipped cream (optional)

1. Whisk eggs in a large mixing bowl with sugar until thick and lemon-colored. Whisk in milk, melted butter, vanilla, cinnamon, and salt. Add bread cubes, and press down with the back of a spoon so they absorb egg mixture. Stir in raisins and candied fruit.

2. Grease the inside of the slow cooker liberally with vegetable oil spray or butter. Spoon mixture into the slow cooker. Cook on High for 1 hour, then reduce the heat to Low and cook for 2 to 3 hours, or until a toothpick inserted into the center comes out clean and an instant-read thermometer inserted into the center of the pudding reads 165°F. Serve hot or at room temperature, with gelato or whipped cream, if using.

Note: The dish can be prepared up to 2 days in advance and refrigerated, tightly covered. Reheat it, covered, in a 350°F oven for 20 to 25 minutes, or until hot.

Variation:
* Substitute chopped dried apricots and chopped dried figs for the candied fruits and raisins.

> While panettone is the bread traditionally used in Italy for bread puddings, it's sometimes hard to find other than at Christmas time in many supermarkets. You can always substitute challah, brioche, or other rich egg breads.

Chocolate Rice Pudding

Riso Nero di Pasqua (pronounced *RI-soh KNEE-ro dee PAS-kah*) is a Sicilian Easter recipe, and since the black color comes from chocolate and not squid ink, this dark rice is a dessert! The inclusion of orange gives it a lighter feel than chocolate alone.

Makes 4 to 6 servings | Prep time: 15 minutes | Minimum cook time: 2¹/₂ hours in a medium slow cooker

1 cup slivered almonds

1 cup Arborio rice

3 cups half-and-half

1 (14-ounce) can sweetened condensed milk

2 tablespoons orange liqueur

6 ounce good quality bittersweet chocolate, chopped

¾ cup finely chopped mixed candied fruit

2 teaspoons grated orange zest

Pinch of salt

½ cup heavy cream

Vanilla ice cream or sweetened whipped cream (optional)

Vegetable oil spray

1. Preheat the oven to 350°F, and line a baking sheet with aluminum foil. Place almonds on the baking sheet and toast nuts for 5 to 7 minutes, or until browned. Remove nuts from the oven, chop coarsely, and set aside.

2. Grease the inside of the slow cooker liberally with vegetable oil spray or butter. Combine rice, half-and-half, sweetened condensed milk, orange liqueur, chocolate, candied fruit, orange zest, and a pinch of salt in the slow cooker. Stir well.

3. Cook on Low for 5 to 7 hours or on High for 2¹/₂ to 3 hours, or until rice is soft and the liquid is thick. Stir in heavy cream. Serve hot, warm, or chilled, topped with ice cream or whipped cream, if using.

Note: The pudding can be prepared up to 1 day in advance and refrigerated, tightly covered with plastic wrap.

Variation:

✻ Substitute Amaretto or other almond-flavored liqueur for the orange liqueur, and omit the orange zest.

> One of the additional health benefits of chocolate is that it has been found to contain catechins—some of the same antioxidants found in green tea. The catechins attack free radicals, which damage cells and are thought to lead to cancer and heart disease. Therefore, eating chocolate, may help to prevent heart disease and cancer—as long as it is eaten in small quantities.

Orange Raisin Rice Pudding

Rice pudding is called *Budino di Riso* (pronounced *buh-DEE-no dee RI-soh*) is a favorite dessert in northern Italy, and this version is rich because whipped cream is folded into a custard base.

Makes 4 to 6 servings | Prep time: 30 minutes | Minimum cook time: 2 hours in a medium slow cooker

1 cup Arborio rice
1 cup granulated sugar, divided
Salt to taste
1½ cups whole milk
½ cup orange marmalade
¼ teaspoon pure vanilla extract
2 large eggs, lightly beaten
½ cup raisins
1 cup heavy whipping cream
Vegetable oil spray

1. Place rice in a sieve, and rinse it well under cold water. Place rice in a 2-quart saucepan with 3 cups water, ½ cup sugar, and salt. Bring to a boil over high heat, and boil for 15 minutes, or until rice is tender. Drain rice.

2. Grease the inside of the slow cooker liberally with vegetable oil spray or butter. Spoon rice into the slow cooker. Combine milk, remaining ½ cup sugar, orange marmalade, vanilla, and eggs in a mixing bowl, and whisk well. Stir mixture into rice, and add raisins. Cook on Low for 4 to 5 hours or on High for 2 to 3 hours, or until custard is set.

3. Remove pudding from the slow cooker, and chill it well. When rice is chilled, place cream in a chilled mixing bowl. Whip cream with an electric mixer on medium until it thickens, then increase the speed to high, and whip cream until stiff peaks form. Fold whipped cream into rice, and serve.

Note: The pudding can be prepared up to 1 day in advance and refrigerated, tightly covered with plastic wrap.

Variation:
✳ Substitute lemon marmalade for the orange marmalade, and substitute chopped dried apricots for the figs.

Fold is the term used for combining a light mixture, such as whipped cream or beaten egg whites, with a denser mixture. In this case, the dense mixture is the rice pudding. The light mixture goes on top, and you insert a rubber spatula into the center of the bowl and push it across the bottom of the bowl. This brings up the dense mixture. Then, turn the bowl a quarter turn, and repeat the motion. The object is to combine the two mixtures without deflating the lighter one.

Poached Figs with Toasted Pine Nuts and Mascarpone

This is a wonderful winter dessert: dried figs rehydrated in red wine flavored with cinnamon and citrus zest, and then topped with creamy cheese and crunchy pine nuts.

Makes 6 to 8 servings | *Prep time: 15 minutes* | *Minimum cook time: 2 hours in a medium slow cooker*

1 (8-ounce) package pound dried Calimyrna figs

2 cups dry red wine

⅔ cup firmly packed light brown sugar

2 (3-inch) cinnamon sticks

2 (3-inch) strips lemon zest

2 (3-inch) strips orange zest

½ cup pine nuts

½ pound mascarpone

1. Stem figs, and cut in half lengthwise. Set aside.

2. Combine wine and brown sugar in the slow cooker, and stir well to dissolve sugar. Add figs, cinnamon sticks, lemon zest, and orange zest to the slow cooker, and stir well. Cook on Low for 4 to 6 hours, or on High for 2 to 3 hours, or until figs are very soft.

3. Remove and discard cinnamon sticks, lemon zest, and orange zest. Transfer figs to a bowl with a slotted spoon. Pour poaching liquid into a saucepan, and bring to a boil over medium-high heat. Cook for 10 minutes, stirring occasionally, or until liquid is reduced by half. Pour liquid over figs, and chill well.

4. While figs cook, place pine nuts in a dry skillet and cook over medium heat, stirring frequently, until brown. Set aside. To serve, spoon mascarpone over figs, and drizzle with poaching liquid. Sprinkle with pine nuts.

Note: The dish can be prepared up to 2 days in advance and refrigerated, tightly covered.

Variation:

✳ Substitute whole dried apricots for the figs.

It's now much easier to find luscious and creamy mascarpone in our supermarkets. But if you can't find it, its taste and texture can be replicated by mixing together 1 (8-ounce) package cream cheese, ¼ pound (1 stick) unsalted butter, and 2 tablespoons sour cream or crème fraîche.

Poached Pears

A simple pear, poached in red wine scented with cinnamon and orange zest, is a perfect ending for a winter meal. Serve some biscotti with it to add crunch.

Makes 4 to 6 servings | Prep time: 15 minutes | Minimum cook time: 2 hours in a medium slow cooker

4 to 6 ripe pears, peeled, halved, and cored
1 cup red wine
¾ cup granulated sugar
1 (3-inch) cinnamon stick
2 (3-inch) strips orange zest

1. Arrange pears in the slow cooker; cut them into quarters, if necessary, to make them fit. Combine wine and sugar in a mixing bowl. Stir well to dissolve sugar, and pour mixture over pears. Add cinnamon stick and orange zest to the slow cooker.

2. Cook on Low for 4 to 5 hours or on High for 2 to 2¹/₂ hours, or until pears are tender when pierced with the point of a knife. Remove and discard cinnamon stick and orange zest. Allow pears to cool in poaching liquid, and serve warm or chilled.

Note: The dish can be prepared up to 2 days in advance and refrigerated, tightly covered.

Variations:
* Substitute sweet Marsala for the red wine, and reduce the amount of sugar to ¹/₂ cup.
* Substitute white wine for the red wine, substitute lemon zest for the orange zest, and omit the cinnamon stick.
* Substitute ripe peaches or white peaches for the pears.

> An easy way to core halved pears and apples is with a melon baller. The shape is efficient, and it leaves a neatly formed round hole.

Baked Stuffed Apples

Baked apples are appreciated in every country, and this Italian version includes some crunchy nuts and flavorful biscotti as part of the stuffing.

Makes 4 to 6 servings | Prep time: 15 minutes | Minimum cook time: 2 hours in a medium slow cooker

½ cup chopped walnuts

4 to 6 baking apples, such as Jonathan and Northern Spy

½ cup crushed almond biscotti

½ cup raisins

2 tablespoons unsalted butter, melted

½ cup dry white wine

¼ cup granulated sugar

1. Preheat the oven to 350°F, and line a baking sheet with aluminum foil. Place walnuts on the baking sheet and toast nuts for 5 to 7 minutes, or until browned. Set aside.

2. Core apples and peel the top half only. Arrange apples in the slow cooker. Combine nuts, biscotti, raisins, and melted butter in a small bowl. Spoon equal portions of mixture into cores of apples.

3. Combine wine and sugar in a mixing bowl, and stir well to dissolve sugar. Spoon mixture over apples.

4. Cook on Low for 4 to 6 hours or on High for 2 to 3 hours, or until apples are tender when pierced with the tip of a knife. Serve hot, at room temperature, or chilled.

Note: The dish can be prepared up to 2 days in advance and refrigerated, tightly covered.

Variation:

✳ Substitute orange marmalade for the sugar, and add 2 (3-inch) strips of orange zest to the slow cooker.

> It's important to peel the top half of the apple. If you don't, the steam builds up inside the skin and the apple tends to fall apart.

Pear and Dried Fruit Compote

During the winter when few fruits are in season, pears are always available, and they go beautifully with a mélange of dried fruits as a topping for gelato.

Makes 6 to 8 servings | Prep time: 15 minutes | Minimum cook time: 1½ hours in a medium slow cooker

1 cup apple cider or apple juice

½ cup granulated sugar

2 tablespoons orange liqueur

1 tablespoon grated orange zest

2 teaspoon grated lemon zest

1 (3-inch) cinnamon stick

2 tablespoons unsalted butter

3 ripe large pears, peeled and cut into 1½-inch dice

½ cup dried apricots, halved

½ cup golden raisins

½ cup chopped dried figs

Vanilla gelato or ice cream

1. Combine apple juice, sugar, orange liqueur, orange zest, lemon zest, and cinnamon stick in a saucepan. Bring to a boil over medium-high heat, stirring to dissolve sugar. Pour mixture into the slow cooker. Stir in butter, pears, apricots, raisins, and figs.

2. Cook on Low for 3 to 5 hours or on High for 1½ to 2 hours, or until pears are tender. Remove and discard cinnamon stick. Serve compote hot or warm over vanilla ice cream.

Note: The dish can be prepared up to 2 days in advance and refrigerated, tightly covered. Reheat it, covered, over low heat until hot, stirring occasionally.

Variation:

✳ Substitute Granny Smith or Golden Delicious apples for the pears, and increase the cooking time by 1 to 2 hours on Low or 30 minutes to 1 hour on High.

There is really quite a difference when you cook with natural apple cider instead of pasteurized apple juice. The cider is far more aromatic, and the apple juice can be sweetened by corn syrup or refined sugar. Always use cider when you can find it.

Index

About Cider Mill Press
Book Publishers

Good ideas ripen with time. From seed to harvest, Cider Mill Press brings fine reading, information, and entertainment together between the covers of its creatively crafted books. Our Cider Mill bears fruit twice a year, publishing a new crop of titles each spring and fall.

BOOK PUBLISHERS

Visit us on the Web at
www.cidermillpress.com
or write to us at
12 Port Farm Road
Kennebunkport, Maine 04046